Leander Whitcomb Munhall

The Highest Critics vs. the Higher Critics

Leander Whitcomb Munhall

The Highest Critics vs. the Higher Critics

ISBN/EAN: 9783744772976

Printed in Europe, USA, Canada, Australia, Japan

Cover: Foto ©Lupo / pixelio.de

More available books at **www.hansebooks.com**

BY THE SAME AUTHOR.

The Lord's Return and Kindred Truth.

Fifth edition. Cloth, 217 pages, $1.

"We know of no work better suited to place in the hands of one who has not made up his mind upon this most important topic."—*Episcopal Recorder*.

"Prepared with a reverent and prayerful spirit. It is certainly an able presentation of the views of those who expect a premillennial advent of Jesus the Christ."—*The Interior*.

Furnishing for Workers.

70th Thousand. It is bound in full flexible leather binding, has 118 pages, can be carried in the pocket without inconvenience, and is only 25 cents per copy.

A prominent business man said of it:

"I would not take five hundred dollars for the copy I have if I could not get another."

"Just the book to carry in the pocket, giving at a bird's-eye glance the passages of Scripture needed to meet an almost endless series of questions, objections, etc., which one constantly hears."—*Book Record*, New York.

THE HIGHEST CRITICS
vs.
THE HIGHER CRITICS

BY

L. W. MUNHALL, M.A., D.D.
EVANGELIST

THIRD EDITION
REVISED AND ENLARGED

NEW YORK: HUNT & EATON
CINCINNATI: CRANSTON & CURTS
1896

Entered according to Act of Congress, in the year 1896, by
L. W. MUNHALL,
In the office of the Librarian of Congress, at Washington, D. C.

TO
MARY THOMAS MUNHALL,

MY WIFE;

A FAITHFUL COMPANION; A DEVOTED MOTHER; A CONSISTENT CHRISTIAN; A WOMANLY WOMAN; AND A SOURCE OF UNFAILING ENCOURAGEMENT IN MY LABORS FOR CHRIST, THIS VOLUME IS MOST AFFECTIONATELY DEDICATED.

L. W. MUNHALL.

CONTENTS.

CHAPTER		PAGE
I.	Who are the Highest Critics?	7
II.	Who are the Higher Critics?	12
III.	Inspiration	19
IV.	Inspiration (Continued)	30
V.	The Bible as a Literary Work	41
VI.	The Bible and Science	55
VII.	The Ethics of the Bible	68
VIII.	The Prophecies of the Bible	79
IX.	The Miracle of the Bible	86

SUPPLEMENTAL DISCUSSION.

X.	The Pentateuch	99
XI.	Job	108
XII.	The Psalms	115
XIII.	Isaiah	136
XIV.	Daniel	150
XV.	Esther	167
XVI.	Work of the Critics Compared	175
XVII.	Scholarship	207
XVIII.	Controversy	217
XIX.	Some Noteworthy Testimonies	221
XX.	The Jew and the Bible	247

INTRODUCTION.

That which is said against the Bible will travel ten times faster and go a great ways further than that which is said in its favor. The secular newspaper press of the country is largely responsible for this. As a class, the managers of our great dailies are either in sympathy with skepticism, or they think that which is said against the Bible is more legitimate news than that which is said in its hehalf. Hence, the preacher who seeks to undermine the "Old Faith," stands a far better chance of being reported, and having his sermons printed, than one who is loyal to the Word of God.

Just now a great deal is being said by these papers favorably to the "Higher Criticism." They publish little or nothing on the other side; and frequently charge those who write and speak against the "Higher Criticism" with indulging in personalities, as though all courtesy and politeness belonged to the "Higher Critics," in this discussion.

There are religious papers of pronounced unorthodox views, and also some with liberalistic tendencies, to which the same criticism may be justly applied.

Then many of the so-called "Higher Critics" are zealous and noisy, and are pushing their opinions and views into notice on all possible occasions.

Then, too, many of them are pursuing the same course as the Unitarians and Universalists in the controversies of twenty-five years ago, by declaring "Scholarship is against the orthodox belief;" "No cultured person believes the Bible to be inerrant;" "We have outgrown the faith of the Fathers;" "The world is moving," etc., etc.

Now, because of these things, the faith and confidence of many are shaken; for the many, in the church of God, have not the time, as some have not the ability, to go deeply into these matters. The object of this volume is to help such people—the many—that they be not "Tossed to and fro and carried about * * * by the sleight of men, in craftiness, after the wiles of error;" that they may be "Rooted and builded up in Him and stablished by faith;" and "Ready always to give answer to every man that asketh a reason concerning the hope that is in them."

No one can be more sensible than the author, of the imperfect character of this work. It has been written while absent from home, while holding from two to four meetings a day, and burdened with a large correspondence and much other work. But the work has been gladly and prayerfully done, with a great desire that it may be honored of God in accomplishing much good, to the glory of His grace.

L. W. M.

GERMANTOWN, PHILADELPHIA, PA., November, 1891.

THE HIGHEST CRITICS
vs.
THE HIGHER CRITICS.

CHAPTER I.

WHO ARE THE HIGHEST CRITICS?

The Highest Critics are the one who spake as "Never man * * * Spake," Jesus Christ, "The Son of the Living God," and He who was sent to "Guide you into all the truth," the Paraclete, the Holy Spirit. These Divine Persons are possessed of infinite attributes. All Christians so believe. Therefore, in the presence of an explicit statement as to the character of the Bible, or the editorship of the same, or any portion thereof, by either of these Persons, all reverent souls bow acquiescently and receive the same with unquestioning faith.

It is not thinkable that they would declare a lie was the truth. I cannot imagine that they would perpetuate an untruth as truth, because it was held traditionally by the Jews. It is monstrous to believe that they would condone a fraud. They are of the truth, they are "the truth," and "no lie is of the truth." If Moses did not write the Pentateuch, or any portion of it, and the Highest Critics declare he did, it would be a lie. It would be none the less a lie even though the Jews held, traditionally, that Moses was the author of these books. The testimony of the Highest Critics is absolutely, unerringly and eternally true, and he who hesitates to receive it, as against all other testimonies, is disloyal to the truth, and will be "Tossed to and fro and carried about with every wind of doctrine, by the sleight of men." Eph. 4 : 14.

There, are, however, not a few in the churches who not only deny the inerrancy of the testimony of the Highest Critics, but, as between their testimony and that of the Higher Critics, they accept the latter.

In a recent meeting of pastors of a certain so-called orthodox denomination in a city not a thousand miles from the capital of this country, the gentleman who was addressing the meeting inquired "If Moses did not write this, why did Jesus Christ say he did?" A pastor in the audience replied: "Because He did not know any better." My honest judgment is that such a statement was blasphemous.

Canon Driver tells us, "You had better not make an issue between the critics and Christ, lest He, too, should go down before them." This statement is very little better than the former. And yet, these men but state the logical outcome of any argument against the inerrancy of the Scriptures, that will not at once give place to the unequivocal testimony of Jesus Christ and the Holy Spirit contrariwise.

Some of the "Higher" Critics set aside the testimony of the Highest Critics for three reasons, viz.:

First. They say: "When Jesus Christ began His ministry, He found the "Traditional views of the matters under discussion, popularly held by the Jews. It was not necessary that He should combat them; and it would, therefore, have been unwise for Him to do so. So He passed them by as not belonging to His plans and work." But this is just what He did not do. He gave them the most positive indorsement by declaring them to be correct, as we shall presently see.

Second. They say: "Jesus and His Apostles were not critics. They were teachers of great ethical principles, and their work was to promulgate these and organize the church." In "The Hebraica" of April, 1889, the case is thus stated: "Christ did not meddle with critical questions connected with the Old Testament, as His mission was of another character. He simply aquiesced in the current views of such questions, as long as they did not affect the nature of that mission. * * * In regard to the Apostles, we cannot, in all cases, adopt their interpretations of the Old Testament, since they were not infallible." It is true that, in the sense the Higher Critic is a critic, they were not, but it is providentially and strikingly true that they did express themselves very fully and clearly upon these very matters in dispute. To impeach their testimony upon the assumption that they were not critics is most audacious.

The learned Canon Liddon says: "The trustworthiness of the Old Testament is, in fact, inseparable from the trustworthiness of the Lord Jesus Christ; and, if we believe that He is the true Light of the world, we shall resolutely close our ears against any suggestions of the falsehood of those Hebrew Scriptures which have received the stamp of His Divine authority."

Third. They say: "The Divine nature in Jesus was dominated by the human during His earthly life, and, therefore, it is unreasonable to believe His teachings to be infallible." They call attention to Luke 2:52, where it is said: "And Jesus advanced in wisdom and stature" (R. V.); "which," they say, "proves conclusively that the Divine nature in Him was subjected to the human; that He did not always possess infinite wisdom." As touching His physical body, we know that it did "advance" (grow) as the bodies of other boys. Identified with His human body was, doubtless, a human mind, susceptible of development, and, as body and mind grew, He became wiser, without doubt, humanly speaking.

That His humanity did again and again manifest itself we have abundant evidence. But, He never taught as a man. His words clearly prove this, "Never man so spake." God said of Him, "The Spirit of the Lord shall rest upon Him, the spirit of wisdom and understanding, the spirit of counsel and might, the spirit of knowledge and of the fear of the Lord" (Isa. 11:1, 2); and, "In Whom are all the treasures of wisdom and knowledge hidden" (Col. 2:3). It is therefore not astonishing that the "Doctors" (Teachers) "That heard Him were amazed at His understanding and His answers" (Luke 2:47), when He was but twelve years old.

They also call attention to what He said when His disciples asked Him, "Tell us when shall these things be? and what shall be the sign of Thy coming, and of the end of the world?" His reply, in part, was, "But of that day and hour knoweth no one, not even the angels of heaven, neither the Son, but the Father only" (Matt. 24: 36).

Let it here be noted, however, that many authorities, some ancient, omit "Neither the Son," but, if these words really belong there, He simply said, as the Divine Teacher, that Jesus the man, humanly speaking, did not know; for as touching His Divinity He said, at another time, "I and the Father are one," therefore, as Deity, He did know.

But these objections against the testimony of Jesus cannot stand, nor those against the testimony of the Apostles, for they wrote by inspiration of the Holy Spirit, and their testimony, therefore, was infallible.

Along with the criticisms of the Highest Critics, I wish, also to emphasize certain self-evident things, belonging properly to this discussion, as possessing far greater value than the opinions and conjectures of the most scholarly of men. By comparisons that may be drawn; by results that are known; by many things that are as evident as the light of day, the eternal truth and unity of the Bible is demonstrated.

CHAPTER II.

WHO ARE THE HIGHER CRITICS?

Presumably they are certain learned and devout men, who gave, or are giving their time almost wholly to an honest, reverent and critical examination of the text of the Scriptures. From such critics the Church of God has nothing to fear, and, indeed, for that matter, from any other kind. But it is sadly true, that they are not all of that sort, as we shall see.

The first criticism bearing upon the Pentateuch, of which we have any knowledge, was in the twelfth century by one Aben Ezra, a Jew. He was followed by Carlstadt, a co-temporary and co-laborer of Luther. Hobbs, the English skeptic, was conspicuous in the seventeenth century for his criticism of these books. Their work met with little favor and made but little headway, even though during these years, beliefs were changing and forming. Toward the close of the seventeenth century, Benedict De Spinoza, a most learned Jew, openly denied the Mosaic Editorship of the Pentateuchal Books, and credited the work to Ezra the Scribe. Less than one hundred and fifty years ago one Jean Astruc, a Frenchman and Roman Catholic, formulated what is called the "Documentary Hypothesis," though this is attributed, by some, to Eichorn. Astruc thought he saw in Genesis evidences of two distinct documents. In some places the Hebrew word

Elohim (God) was used; in others, the word Jehovah (Lord). He concluded that there must have been two writers. Therefore, Moses was not the writer but the compiler of this book.

Then some German critics taught that the entire Pentateuch was a sort of "crazy quilt" arrangement of a lot of anonymous documents that Moses found lying around loose, and put together. This is called the "Fragmentary Theory." The striking and remarkable unity of these books compelled an abandonment of this theory.

The "Edition Theory" was the next in order. The Pentateuch was amended so as to include the book of Joshua and, of course, christened "The Hexateuch." The Editor is the "great unknown": but there was one, of that they were certain; and he, having the original Elohist document before him, so amended it, and added to it from materials at hand, that we have the—"The Hexateuch."

The German scholar, Hupfeld, in 1853, formulated the "Compilation Theory." He not only has an Elohist writer and Editor, but a Jahvist and a second Elohist; and now his pupils have still another called the "Priestly Elohist," and many others yet to be heard from. His followers insist that the Hexateuchal Books were not written and put into their present form until after the return of the Children of Israel from the Babylonish captivity, about B. C. 444; and that Moses, therefore, had nothing whatever to do with the authorship or editorship of the Pentateuch. They also teach that

Isaiah did not write the last twenty-seven chapters of the Prophecy bearing his name; that David wrote few or none of the Psalms; that Job and Jonah are unhistorical; and that Esther and Daniel are uninspired and fictitious.

In 1836 Ferdinand Christian Baur, of Tubingen, in Wurtenburg, came to the front as leader of the Destructionists, and, in a most audacious and insolent manner, attacked the integrity of the New Testament.

The best (worst) this destructive school could do was to conclude that the first three Gospels were written shortly after the destruction of Jerusalem by the Romans, under Titus. That the Gospel of John, the Revelation and the Epistles of John were written by an immediate disciple of John. That the Acts were suspected of being a partisan version of history. That Romans, First and Second Corinthians, Galatians and Philippians are genuine. Colossians, First Thessalonians and Philemon were regarded with a preponderance of favorable judgment. Hebrews and First Peter were recognized as belonging to the first century. James was treated as anonymous and an early literary fragment of Jewish Christianity. Ephesians, Second Thessalonians, First and Second Timothy, Titus, Jude and Second Peter, or a total of eight books out of twenty-seven, or fifteen pages out of a total of two hundred and eight, they shelved, or thought they did. But did they?

The chief result of the labors of these men and

their followers was to unspiritualize the evangelical churches in Germany, Switzerland and Holland, in large measure, and give them over to Rationalizing. Otherwise, their labors were for naught. But the New Testament still remains in its integrity, and is believed and honored by twice as many intelligent and godly people as in Baur's day.

At the present time the Old Testament is the subject of criticism. Kuenen and Wellhausen on "The Continent;" Robertson and George Adam Smith and others in England and Scotland; and Profs. Briggs and Harper in this country, are considered leaders of the crusade against the integrity of the Old Testament.

They, like former and older critics, may make notoriety for themselves and a stir in the churches; but fifty years hence their influence will be no more felt than that of the Tubingen school, and the Old Testament will still remain in all its present strength and beauty, potential for greater good than ever before.

The present agitation enables many enemies of the Bible to come to the front. Therefore we ought to be careful to ascertain who it is that speaks and writes.

Some apparently only seek to destroy the faith of the church in the Bible as an infallible guide. They parade and magnify the apparent discrepancies and errors, and seldom, if ever, give the reconciliations and verifications that have been clearly proven. Nor do they point out the proofs of the integrity and inerrability of the Scriptures. Their efforts seem to be to discredit them. These are dishonest critics—destructionists.

He who says "The Bible is no better than a 'Mass Book' for stopping a bullet; and not as good as 'Holy Water' for putting out a fire," is an irreverent critic; be he never so religious, honest and scholarly. He is sure to play into the hands of the enemies of God's Word.

The unspiritual critic is more likely to be wrong than right in his conclusions. The man who deliberately addresses himself to the work of criticising the Bible, as he would criticise any other book, without its subtle and transforming power in his heart and life, and depending upon the Holy Spirit who was sent to guide us into all truth (see John 16:13) to help him, will most surely become entangled in the intricacies of his own thoughts, be he the most learned of men. God's Word says: "Now the natural man receiveth not the things of the spirit of God, for they are foolishness unto him, and he cannot know them, because they are spiritually judged (or examined)." 1 Cor. 2:14. And this is true for the simple reason that God's thoughts are as much higher than man's as the heaven is above the earth. See Isa. 55:9.

There is not a man in the pulpits of orthodox Christendom, or in a theological or editorial chair, who is unscriptural in the doctrines of inspiration, original sinfulness, atonement, repentance, faith, justification, regeneration and the new birth, sanctification, resurrection, judgment and final retribution for unbelievers—and there are hundreds of such—who does not assume to be a "Higher Critic," or, in hearty sympathy with any and every criticism of the "Higher Critics," that in any sense questions the integrity of the Bible. I personally know scores of these gentlemen. They do not preach the "gospel of God," because they do not believe it. They do not "Reprove, rebuke, exhort with all long suffering and teaching." Their pulpits are but "lecture platforms," and their churches but little if any better than social clubs for the promotion of some other things than the king's business. Sinners do not throng their altars inquiring the way of life and salvation, and the work appointed unto the church by Jesus Christ is not done by them. These are the men who, as a rule, are now most vehement and noisy in urging the claims of the Higher Criticism.

Therefore we need to be careful to ascertain who is the "Higher Critic" we are following. There be blind leaders of the blind. And if the blind lead the blind, both shall fall into the ditch. (Matt. 15: 14.)

We ought also, always to remember that the wisest and most learned man is a fallible being, can only "know in part," and "see through a glass darkly." "Therefore we should never try to harmonize the plain teachings of the Bible with the views or opinions of men; but if we attempt any reconciliation, let it be of men's views to the Word of God; and, if we fail, let us conclude that these men are mistaken in their conclusions. "Let God be found true, but every man a liar." (Rom. 3:4.) The creeds of Christendom agree that "The Bible is the only infallible rule of faith and practice." Therefore, let us ascertain if the "Higher Critics" agree with the Highest. If they do, let us thankfully accept their help. If not, let us pass them by.

CHAPTER III.

INSPIRATION.

The so called "Higher Critics," to a man, so far as I know, disbelieve the doctrine of verbal inspiration, although for more than one thousand years the Church entertained no other view. Prof. B. B. Warfield, of Princeton Theological Seminary, said in an article on "The Westminster Doctrine of Inspiration," recently published in the New York Independent. "Doubtless enough has been said to show that the confession teaches precisely the doctrine which is taught in the private writings of the framers, which was also the general Protestant doctrine of the time, and not of that time only or of the Protestants only; for despite the contrary assertion that has recently become tolerably current essentially this doctrine of inspiration has been the doctrine of the Church of all ages and of all names."

They have various theories of inspiration: Some say, "The thoughts only of the penmen were inspired." Some say, "They were only partially inspired." But they are very indefinite in their statements of the extent of this inspiration. Some say, "There were different degrees of inspiration," and they use the difference between illumination and inspiration to prove it. Some say, "At one time they were inspired in the supervision of the work they did;" at another, "In the view they took of the work they were called upon to do;" and at another, "In directing the work." But in all these views they are at sea, and leave all who trust to their pilotage at sea as to the exact character and limitations of inspiration. They sometimes talk of "Dynamic" inspiration, but their efforts to explain what they mean by this term are exceedingly vague and misty. But the popular and current theory now is that the "Concept" is inspired. But no one attempts to tell what the "Concept" is; indeed, I doubt if any of these critics know.

The one thing they are emphatic about and united upon is, that the Bible is not verbally inspired. The noisy ones will tell you that "No scholar believes in the theory of verbal inspiration." In this they bear false witness. Another expression in common use among them is this: "Such belief drives men into infidelity!" And yet not one of them ever knew of a case. This class, with as much care and evident satsifaction as an infidel, hunts out the apparent contradictions and errors in the authorized and revised versions of the Bible, and holding them up to the public gaze exultingly declare: "Here is conclusive evidence that the Bible is not verbally inspired." Many of these gentlemen are dishonest because, *First*, they know that most of these apparent errors and contradictions were long ago satisfactorily answered, even to the silencing of infidel scoffers; and, *Second*, they know that no one believes that the transcribers, translators, and revisers were inspired. The doctrine of verbal inspiration is simply this: The original writings, *ipsissima verba*, came through the penmen direct from God; and these gentlemen are only throwing dust into the air when they rail against verbal inspiration and attempt to disprove it by pointing out the apparent errors and discrepancies of the authorized and revised texts.

But some say, "Since we do not have the original writings, what is the use of insisting upon the doctrine of verbal inspiration?" I answer, there are two sufficient reasons: *First*. If the original writings were not inspired of God verbally, then we have no Word of God. *Second*. Is there no difference between an inexact copy of an inerrable record and a faulty copy of an uncertain record? I think there is. I rejoice that, notwithstanding the "Higher Critics" long ago discovered, or they thought they did, 30,000 various readings in the different manuscripts, yet, as Cardinal Wiseman says, "In all this mass, although every attainable source has been exhausted; although the fathers of every age have been gleaned for their readings; although the versions of every nation, Arabic, Syriac, Coptic, Armenian and Ethiopian, have been ransacked for their renderings; although manuscripts of every age, from the sixteenth century upwards to the third, and of every country, have been again and again visited by industrious swarms to rifle them of their treasures; although, having exhausted the stores of the West, critics have traveled, like naturalists into distant lands, to discover new specimens, have visited, like

Scholz or Sebastian, the recesses of Mount Athos, or the unexplored libraries of the Egyptian and Syrian deserts, yet has nothing been discovered, no, not one single various reading, which can throw doubt upon any passage before considered certain or decisive in favor of any important doctrine, * * * These various readings, almost without an exception, leave untouched the essential parts of any sentence, and only interfere with points of secondary importance, the insertion or omission of an article or conjunction, the more accurate grammatical construction, or the forms rather than the substance of words."

The skeptics have been discomfited in every assault at this point. The more recent investigations of Tregelles, Tischendorf, and other most learned and able critics, have made the intrenched position held by the orthodox church through the ages, impregnable; so that we can say with the learned Gaussen, "Not only was the Scripture inspired on the day God caused it to be written, but that we possess this Word inspired eighteen hundred years ago; and that we may, while holding our sacred text in one hand, and in the other all the readings collected by the learned in seven hundred manuscripts, exclaim with thankfulness, I hold in my hands my Father's Testament, the eternal word of my God!"

There is no doubt in my own mind but that many of the Transcribers, Translators, and Revisers had a large measure of illumination in doing their work. This is clearly seen in the pureness of the texts we have. It surely would have been otherwise had not God vouchsafed guidance and help, in the important work of transmitting His Word to succeeding generations.

God is an intelligent Being. He has always treated man as a sentient and reasoning creature. In the Bible we have a revelation, to man, of God's mind and purposes concerning certain things. But the Bible is composed of words. These words express thoughts. It is not possible to express thoughts apart from words, or even to entertain them. If verbal inspiration is not true, then the Bible is not from God at all: it is a human composition.

At the last analysis, any doctrine of inspiration save verbal, means a denial of the supernaturalness of the Bible. This is logically inevitable. Hence those who deny the fundamental doctrines of the Bible that are unpleasant to the natural man, are most determined and sometimes savage in their efforts to destroy the faith of the Church in the doctrine of verbal inspiration. This, to my mind, is strikingly significant.

There are those, it is true, who are firm believers in all the fundamental doctrines of grace, who yet deny the fact of verbal inspiration, but when these gentlemen talk about inspiration they mean illumination. All men have illumination. "There is a light which lighteth every man that cometh into the world." But few men have ever been inspired. Here is a case of inspiration: "Ah! Lord God! behold, I cannot speak, for I am a child. But the

Lord said unto me, say not I am a child, for thou shalt go to all that I shall send thee, and whatsoever I command thee thou shalt speak. Be not afraid of their faces, for I am with thee to deliver thee, saith the Lord. Then the Lord put forth his hand and touched my mouth. And the Lord said unto me, Behold, I have put my words in thy mouth." (Jer. 1:6-9.)

But what say the Highest Critics on this subject?

Jesus Christ said: "David himself said in the Holy Spirit." (Mark 12:36.) Notice, He does not say David thought, but David himself *said*. Turn to 2 Sam. 23:2, and we will find additional information to this case. David said: "The spirit of the Lord spake by me, and His word was upon my tongue." He did not say "The spirit gave me a concept," or " His thought was in my mind," but, "The spirit of the Lord *spake* by me and His *word* was upon my *tongue*."

The Holy Spirit said: "All scripture is given by inspiration of God." The word rendered scripture in this passage is *graphé*. It means writing. The writing is composed of words. What else is this but verbal inspiration?

But the critics say: "The revised version renders this passage. "Every scripture inspired of God is also profitable." It may appear presumptuous in me to say so, but since the learned men who gave us the Revised Version have not claimed infallibility for themselves, and this is a free country, I have no hesitation in saying that these gentlemen have erred in this case, in my humble judgment. I think so for the following reasons: *First.* It is tautological. *Second.* It is a violation of the laws of Greek syntax. Bishop Middleton challenged the production of a single instance in the compass of the whole Greek language where such a violent divulsion of two adjectives connected and standing as they are in 2 Tim. 3: 16, could be found and justified. The challenge remains unanswered. Dr. John Pye Smith attempted to produce an instance, but was overthrown by Dr. S. P. Tregelles.

Third. The Greek fathers certainly knew their own language better than the Revisers. Clement of Alexandria says, "The Apostle calls the Scripture inspired of God." Origen says, "Every Scripture is *theopneustic,* and is profitable." Gregory of Nyssa says, "Every Scripture is, by Paul, said to be inspired of God." Chrysostom says, "Every Scripture is, by the Apostle, said to be inspired of God." So also say Theodoret, Basil and Cyril.

Fourth. In 1 Tim. 4: 4, Paul says, "Every creature of God is good and nothing to be refused;" and, in Heb. 4: 13 we are told that "All things are naked and opened (exposed) to the eyes of Him with whom we have to do." These two passages are absolutely identical in form and construction as 2 Tim. 2: 16. The Revisers left these two passages unchanged. And why? Because if they had changed them as they did 2 Tim. 2: 16, they would have made absolute nonsense of them and a laughing-stock of themselves.

Fifth. The Revisers condemned their own rendering by putting the authorized text in the margin. "All Scripture is given by inspiration of God, and is profitable," etc., is not the equivalent of "ALL Scripture inspired of God is also profitable," etc.

Sixth. By the revised rendering each person is authorized to decide for him or herself just what Scripture is inspired. This is just the liberty many of the Higher Critics take. They accept what supports their pet views and theories and throw the rest away. Every man becomes a law unto himself in the matter.

Seventh. The revised rendering has been condemned by a great many of the best scholars on earth. Bishops Moberly and Wordsworth, Archbishop Trench and others of the Revision Committee disclaimed any responsibility for the rendering. Dean Burgon pronounced it the "Most astonishing as well as calamitous literary blunder of the age." The distinguished critic, Dr. Schrivener, calls it "A blunder such as makes itself hopelessly condemned." It was condemned by Dr. Tregelles, the only man ever pensioned by the British Government for scholarship, as it was condemned by the scholars of Reformation times.

But for all this, the Revised Version does not materially change the teaching of the text respecting verbal inspiration; for, if it were correct, it is bound to the writings which Timothy had been taught from "wee" childhood, which are declared to be "sacred" and "Able to make * * * wise unto salvation through faith which is in Christ Jesus."

Of these "Sacred" writings the Holy Spirit says: "For no prophecy ever came by the will of man: but men spake from God, being moved by the Holy Ghost. (2 Peter 1:21.) The word "Prophecy" in this passage, is not limited to the foretelling of events. It signifies the revelation of the mind of God in human language. It is asserted, unequivocally, that certain men "Spake (not thought) from God, being moved by the Holy Ghost."

We are told in Luke 24: 27, that Jesus Christ, "Beginning from Moses and from all the Prophets * * * interpreted to them (the disciples) in all the Scriptures the things concerning Himself." We are here informed that Moses and certain other men called Prophets, humanly speaking, were the authors of that which Timothy was instructed in, called the "Holy Scriptures," or "Sacred Writings," which were written and spoken of God by the Holy Spirit.

Now let us turn to some of these books and ascertain what the writers said concerning the matter under consideration. Ex. 4: 10–12: "And Moses said unto the Lord, I am not eloquent (a man of words), neither heretofore nor since thou hast spoken unto thy servant: for I am slow of speech, and of a slow tongue. And the Lord said unto him, Who hath made man's mouth? * * * Now therefore go and I will be with thy mouth, and teach thee what thou shalt speak." Ex. 34: 27: "And the Lord said unto Moses, write thou these words: for after the tenor of these words I have made a covenant with thee, and with Israel." Deut. 4: 2: "Ye shall not add unto the word which I command you, neither shall ye diminish from it." Deut. 18: 20: "But the prophet which shall speak a word presumptuously in my name, which I have not commanded him to speak, * * * that prophet shall die."

In the five books of Moses, in the books called historical, and books included under the general title of the Psalms, such expressions as the following occur hundreds of times, viz: "Thus saith the Lord;" "The Lord said;" "The Lord spake;" "The Lord hath spoken;" "The Lord promised;" "The saying of the Lord;" and "The word of the Lord." There is no other thought expressed in these books concerning inspiration than that the writers spoke and wrote the very words that God gave them.

Turning to the books called prophetical we find Isaiah saying, Hear the word of the Lord (Isa. 1: 10); and no fewer than twenty times does he explicitly declare that his writings are the "Words of the Lord." Almost one hundred times does Jeremiah say, "The word of the Lord came unto me," or declare he was uttering the "Words of the Lord," and the "Word of the Living God." Ezekiel says that his writings are the "Words of God," quite sixty times. Here is a sample:—"Son of man, all my words that I shall speak unto thee receive in thine heart, and hear with thine ears. And go get thee to them of the captivity, unto the children of thy people, and speak unto them, and tell them thus saith the Lord God" (Ezek. 3:10, 11). Daniel said, "And when I heard the voice of His words" (Dan. x:9). Hosea said, "The word of the Lord" (Hosea 1:1). "The word of the Lord that came to Joel (Joel 1:1). Amos said, "Hear the word of the Lord" (Amos 3:1). Obadiah said, "Thus saith the Lord God" (Oba. 1:1). "The word of the Lord came unto Jonah" (Jon. 1:1). "The word of the Lord that came to Micah" (Micah 1:1). Nahum said, "Thus saith the Lord" (Nah. 1:12). Habakkuk wrote, "The Lord answered me and said" (Hab. 2:2). "The word of the Lord which came to Zephaniah". (Zeph. 1:1). "Came the word of the Lord to Haggai the prophet" (Hag. 1:1). "Came the word of the Lord unto Zechariah" (Zech. 1:1). "The word of the Lord to Israel by Malachi" (Mal. 1:1). And in this last of the Old Testament books is it twenty-four times said "Thus saith the Lord."

CHAPTER IV.

INSPIRATION (Continued.)

When we turn to the New Testament Scriptures we find these words of Jesus: "But when they deliver you up, be not anxious how or what ye shall speak. For it is not ye that speak, but the Spirit of your Father that speaketh in you." (Matt. 10 : 19, 20.) "And when they lead you to the judgment, and deliver you up, be not anxious beforehand what ye shall speak: but whatsoever shall be given you in that hour, that speak ye; for it is not ye that speak, but the Holy Ghost." (Mark 13 : 11.) "And when they bring you before the synagogues, and the rulers, and the authorities, be not anxious how or what ye shall answer, or what ye shall say: for the Holy Spirit shall teach you in that very hour what ye ought to say." (Luke 12 : 11, 12.) "Settle it therefore in your hearts, not to meditate beforehand how to answer; for I will give you a mouth and wisdom, which all your adversaries shall not be able to withstand or to gainsay." (Luke 21 : 14, 15.) In these passages we are plainly taught that the Apostles and certain of the disciples were to be inspired to speak certain things. This same inspiration included all the disciples on the day of Pentecost, for they were all with one accord in one place. * * * And they were all filled with the Holy Spirit, and began to speak with other tongues as the Spirit gave them utterance." (Acts

2 : 1, 4.) The multitude that heard "Marvelled, saying, Behold, are not all these which speak Galileans? And how hear we every man in our own language? * * * we do hear them speaking in our tongues the mighty works of God." (Acts 2 : 7, 11.)

Luke introduces the Gospel bearing his name with this statement: "Forasmuch as many have táken in hand to draw up a narrative concerning those matters which have been fulfilled (fully established) among us, even as they delivered them unto us, which from the beginning were eye-witnesses and ministers of the word, it seemed good to me also, having traced the course of all things accurately from the first, to write unto thee in order, most excellent Theophilus: that thou mightest know the certainty concerning the things (Greek words) wherein thou was instructed (or literally, which thou wast taught by word of mouth).

The opening words of Revelation are these, "The Revelation of Jesus Christ, which God gave him to show unto his servants, even the things which must shortly come to pass; and he sent and signified it by his angel unto his servant John; who bare witness of the word of God, and of the testimony of Jesus Christ, even of all things that he saw. Blessed is he that readeth, and they that hear the words of the prophecy, and keep the things which are written therein; for the time is at hand." (Rev. 1: 1–3.)

When we examine Paul's writings we find these most explicit statements: "Which things also we speak, not in words which man's wisdom teacheth, but which the Spirit teacheth." (1 Cor. 2: 13.) "And for this cause we also thank God without ceasing, that, when ye received from us the word of the message, *even the word* of God, ye accepted it not as the word of men, but, as it is in truth, the word of God." (1 Thess. 2: 13.) "But unto the married I give charge, *yea* not I, but the Lord." (1 Cor. 7: 10.) Peter bears this testimony to the inspiration of Paul's writings: "Even as our beloved brother Paul also, according to the wisdom given to him, wrote unto you; as also in all his epistles, speaking in them of these things; wherein are some things hard to be understood, which the ignorant and unsteadfast wrest, as *they do* also the other scriptures." (2 Peter 3: 15, 16.) Two things are herein affirmed, viz.: First, Paul's epistles were known, at that time, in all the churches; and, Second, they are equally authoritative with all the other Scriptures.

Peter said, "This is now, beloved, the second epistle that I write unto you: and in both of them I stir up your sincere mind by putting you in remembrance; that ye should remember the words which were spoken before by the holy prophets, and the commandment of the Lord and Savior through your apostles.' (2 Peter 3: 1, 2.) Peter here explicitly declares that his own writings are of equal authority with Paul's and the other apostles, and the prophets.

And so the Bible, uniformly, from first to last,

teaches the doctrine of verbal inspiration. It is the Word of God. This is the invariable testimony of the Highest Critics. They never, in a single instance, say that the thoughts of the writers of the Bible were inspired; or, that these writers had a "Concept." Only the "Higher Critics" talk in this way. The "Highest Critics" call the Scriptures—"The Oracles of God" (Rom. 3:2.); "The Word of God" (Luke 8:11); "The Word of the Lord" (Acts 13:48); "The Word of Life" (Phil. 2:16); "The Word of Christ" (Col. 3:16); "The Word of Truth" (Eph. 1:13); "The Word of Faith" (Rom. 10:8); and, by these and similar statements do they declare, more than *two thousand times*, that the Bible is the Word of God,—that the words are God-breathed, are inspired. (Theopneustia.)

It is doubtless true, as a rule, that God operated through the thoughts and wills of those who were inspired to speak and write. I think this is apparent in the different characteristics of those who wrote the Bible, as seen in their writings; but, it was not always the case, indeed in some cases, the inspiration was beyond the thought and independent of it, and, in immediate conflict with the will. The dumb ass had no "Concept," but "The Lord opened the mouth of the ass, and she said unto Balaam, What have I done unto thee, that thou hast smitten me these three times? And the ass said unto Balaam, Am not I thine ass, upon which thou hast ridden all thy life long unto this day? Was I ever wont to do so unto thee?" (Numb. 22:28, 30.)

"But a certain one of them, Caiaphas, being high priest that year, said unto them, Ye know nothing at all, nor do ye take account that it is expedient for you that one man should die for the people, and that the whole nation perish not. Now this he said not of himself; but being high priest that year, he prophesied that Jesus should die for the nation: and not for the nation only, but that he might also gather together into one the children of God that are scattered abroad" (John 11:49-52.). This is a case of inspiration independent of thought—"Now this he said not of himself."

In the case of the disciples on the "Day of Pentecost" we have inspiration above human thought. They spake "With other tongues as the Spirit gave them utterance." Speaking languages of which they had no knowledge, so that the multitude "Were confounded because that every man heard them speaking in his own language."

Balaam was compelled to speak against his will. He said: "Lo, I am come unto thee; have I now any power at all to say any thing? the word that God putteth in my mouth, that shall I speak." (Where are the dynamics in this case?) He did his very utmost to curse the Israelites, but as often as he tried it, he blessed them. Balak at last said "Neither curse them at all, nor bless them at all." But Balaam answered, "Told not I thee, saying, All the Lord speaketh, that I must do." (Numb. 22:38; 23:26.)

Even independent of any living agency, God wrote

the words of the law upon the tables of stone, in the top of smoke-wreathed and fire-crowned Sinai; and caused a hand to stand forth and write upon the wall of the festal hall, the words "Mene, Mene, Tekel, Upharsin," to the astonishment and consternation of Belshazzar and his one thousand lords.

At the baptism of Jesus there was heard, "A voice from heaven, saying, "This is my beloved Son, in whom I am well pleased." (Matt. 3: 17.)

Amid the dazzling splendors of the Transfiguration scene, there came "A voice out of the cloud, which said, "This is my beloved Son, in whom I am well pleased; hear ye him. (Matt. 17: 5.)

When Saul of Tarsus was smitten, while on his way to Damascus, "The Lord said (unto him), I am Jesus, whom thou persecutest: Arise and go into the city, and it shall be told thee what thou must do. And the men which journeyed with him stood speechless, hearing a voice, but seeing no man." (Acts 9: 5-7.)

No "Inspiration of Superintendence;" or of "Elevation;" or of "Direction;" or of "Suggestion," can by any possible means explain these last cases.

Dr. Adam Clark once said: "A good man could not have written the Bible, and a bad man would not have written it." Another has said: "Man couldn't have written the Bible if he would, and wouldn't have written it if he could."

In these two statements are three self-evident truths. *First.* Over and over again the Bible tells us that God the Holy Spirit was its author. Now, if man was its author, he was a liar, and consequently not a good man.

Second. A bad man would not have written the Bible if he could, for the simple reason it tells him what he is. It speaks of unchristian men as "Abominable Branches," "Ashes under the feet," "Bad Fishes," "Beasts," "The Blind," "Brass and Iron," "Briers and Thorns," "Bulls of Bashan," "Carcasses trodden under feet," "Chaff," "Clouds without water," "Corn Blasted," "Corrupt Trees," "Deaf Adders," "Dogs," "Dross," "Early dew that passeth away," "Evil Figs," "Fading Oaks," "Fiery Oven," "Fire of Thorns," "Fools building upon sand," "Fuel of fire," "Gardens without water," "Goats," "Grass upon the Housetops," "Green-bay trees," "Green Herbs," "Heath in the Desert," "Horses rushing into battle," "Idols," "Lions greedy of prey," "Melting Wax," "Morning Clouds," "Moth-eaten garments," "Passing Whirlwinds," "Potsherds," "Raging waves of the sea," "Reprobate Silver," "Scorpions," "Serpents," "Smoke," "Stony Ground," "Stubble," "Swine," "Tares," "Troubled Sea," "Visions of the Night," "Wandering Stars," "Wayward Children," "Wells without Water," "Whited Sepulchres," "Wild Asses' Colts." In the nature of the case it is not thinkable that any man would write such things against himself. So very true is this that it is most difficult to get unchristian men, as a rule, to even read the book with anything like carefulness, or to go to church lest they hear God's estimate of them.

Third. Man could not have written the Bible if he would. I can by application and study fathom the depths of the writings of the wisest and most learned of men. We occupy, in some respects, the same plane of possibilities. We are men. "Canst thou by searching find out God?" "O the depth of the riches both of the wisdom and the knowledge of God! how unsearchable are His judgments, and His ways past tracing out!" Rom. 11:33.

Prof. Gaussen says: "The theory of a Divine revelation, in which you would have the inspiration of the thoughts, without the inspiration of the language, is so inevitably irrational that it cannot be sincere, and proves false even to those who propose it."

Dr. Charles Hodge says, "The inspiration of the Scriptures extends to the words."

Prof. A. A. Hodge says, "The line can never rationally be drawn between the thoughts and words of Scripture * * * That we have an inspired Bible, and a verbally inspired one, we have the witness of God Himself."

Charles Spurgeon says: "We cannot refrain from uttering our growing conviction that the Scriptures possess a verbal as well as plenary inspiration."

Dean Burgon, a member of the Revision Committee, and a man of vast learning, says, You cannot dissect inspiration into substance and form. As for thoughts being inspired, apart from the words which give them expression, you might as well talk of a tune without notes, or a sum without figures. No such theory of inspiration is even intelligible. It is as illogical as it is worthless, and cannot be too sternly put down."

Napoleon the Great once said, "Book unique, where the mind finds a moral beauty before unknown, and an idea of the Supreme superior even to that which creation suggests! Who but God could produce that type, that ideal of perfection, equally exclusive and original?"

With the learned Bishop Ryle I say: Give me the plenary verbal theory with all its difficulties, rather than the doubt. I accept the difficulties, and humbly wait for their solution; but while I wait I am standing on a rock."

Yonder, upon the bosom of the granite hills, is a fountain. By some unknown and untraceable conduit it is connected with some greater fountain amid the glaciers and eternal snows of loftier heights. From its subterranean depths and inexhaustible source it pours forth its floods of pure, clear, life-giving water. Stretching away from the base of these solemn hills, far beyond the horizon, is an arid, desert waste. Evidences of life are but few in all its vast expanse, and it lies desolate under storm and calm. But enterprising men gather the floods of this fountain into a great reservoir, and thence carry it, by pipes and ditches, abroad over the dusty plain; and soon teeming fields, throbbing with life, everywhere greet the eye; and happy homes and sunny-faced children are seen; and we hear the song of the milk-maid and the shout of the plow-boy, and all is beautiful, peaceful and serene.

But, suppose someone shall, in the midnight hour, climb to that fountain, and put into its waters that which is poisonous, until through its channels death flows out to those fruitful fields and happy homes; and men and women die; and the beasts of the field perish; and the harvests are unreaped; and that which is bright and beautiful fades; and death dominates all the scene. Would he not be an enemy of his kind who did this awful thing? indeed, a fiend incarnate?

The Word of God is a fountain, connected, how, you and I know not, with the fountain of perennial youth in the heart of The Eternal. The Church of God is but a reservoir for receiving these life-giving floods; and forth from this reservoir these waters are to constantly flow, to make glad the waste places.

Some go through the conduit of the Westminster Confession of Faith, others through the Augsburg, Savoy, and Heidelberg Confessions, and yet others through the Thirty-Nine and the Twenty-Five Articles. No matter how these floods are conducted, so they reach the desolate places of earth. Our business is to keep the conduits clean and unobstructed, and let the waters flow on forever.

I have looked into these waters and seen myself reflected to the very innermost and uttermost, saw myself as God sees me, polluted and defiled; needy, perishing and dying. I plunged me into their crystal depths, and was washed from all the stain and defilement of sin. My thirsty soul drank long and deep of the life-giving flood; my thirst was slaked and I was satisfied, and ever more shall be. Millions, beside, have had similar experiences.

"The Waters of Life" as they have flowed into the dark, desolate and waste places of the earth, where grew but "Fornication, uncleanness, lasciviousness, idolatry, sorcery, enmities, strife, jealousies, wraths, factions, divisions, heresies, envyings, revelings, drunkenness, and such like," the fruits of the flesh, have caused them to "Rejoice and blossom as the rose," and bring forth luxuriant and abundant harvests of "Love, joy, peace, long-suffering, kindness, goodness, faithfulness, meekness, temperance, virtue, patience and knowledge," the fruits of the Spirit.

Surely he who poisons the waters of this life-giving fountain, by casting in doubts; or, pollutes them with his mystifying opinions and views, is the enemy of his kind.

CHAPTER V.

THE BIBLE AS A LITERARY WORK.

I desire to call attention to certain structural evidences and proofs, by comparisons, of the Divine Authorship of the Bible, all of which I hold prove, to a demonstration, its supernaturalness.

I occasionally meet a young man who says: "The Bible is an outworn and outlived book, possessing little or no literary merit, and little thought of and used by scholarly men."

Over against this and similar remarks, often heard now-a-days, I wish to place the testimonies of a few illustrious men, who certainly were competent to speak upon the subject. Sir Walter Scott said as he neared the end of his earthly journey, "There is but one Book." Patrick Henry once said, "There is a Book worth all other books." John Adams said, "The Bible is the best Book in the world." Goethe said, "It is a belief in the Bible which has served me as the guide of my literary life." Daniel Webster once said, "If there is anything in my style or thoughts to be commended, the credit is due to my kind parents in instilling into my mind an early love of the Scriptures."

Sir W. Jones, the jurist and Orientalist, the most accomplished scholar of his day in England, said: "The Scriptures contain, independently of a Divine origin, more true sublimity, more exquisite beauty, purer morality, more important history, and finer strains both of poetry and eloquence, than could be collected within the same compass from all other books that were ever composed in any age or in any idiom."

Sir Matthew Hale once said, "I have been acquainted somewhat with men and books, and have had long experience in learning, and in the world; there is no book like the Bible for excellent learning, wisdom, and use; and it is want of understanding in them that think or speak otherwise."

Boyle, the natural philosopher, said, "The Bible is indeed among books what the diamond is among stones, the most precious and sparkling; the most apt to scatter light, and yet the solidest and the most proper to make impressions."

Baron Humboldt said: "The epic or historical parts (of the Old Testament) are marked by a graceful simplicity, almost more unadorned than those of Herodotus, and most true to nature."

Coleridge said: "Intense study of the Bible will keep any man from being vulgar in point of style."

Prof. Huxley says of the Bible: "It is written in the noblest and purest English, and abounds in exquisite beauties of a merely literary form."

Examine carefully the language of the Book; and, as surely as you are competent to judge correctly, and are honest, you will conclude that it is incomparable. Its smoothness, beauty and sententiousness of expression is unique. Someone has said, "It would require a trip-hammer to knock a word out of any sentence John Milton ever wrote." Much more is such a statement true of the Bible. Turn to the opening chapter and read: "In the beginning God created the heaven and the earth. And the earth was waste and void; and darkness was upon the face of the waters. And God said, Let there be light: and there was light. And God saw the light, that it was good: And God divided the light from the darkness. And God called the light Day and the darkness he called Night. And there was evening and there was morning, one day." And so as you read you will agree with the infidel Rousseau, "I must confess the majesty of the Scriptures strikes me with astonishment."

Anyhow, I know no man wrote those opening sentences. It's his habit to amplify and write verbosely. Hence, writing of "Beginning," he would have enlarged and given us an octavo volume on Cosmos; and coming to speak of "Light," he certainly would have given us an extended treatise on the subject. Usually, he is very fond of writing on subjects of which he has little or no knowledge.

POETRY.

It is often said: "There are no poems in

the Bible." It is true that the Hebrews were not of a poetic mind or disposition. But where in the libraries of the wide world can be found poetry comparable to some of the Psalms, portions of Isaiah, Ezekiel and Daniel? of Job and the Revelation? What of "The Songs of Moses, of Miriam, of Debora and of Mary? Where in the languages of earth is there anything that will equal the following for real poetic beauty and expression?

"Thy glory, O Israel, is slain upon thy high places!
How are the mighty fallen!
Tell it not in Gath,
Publish it not in the streets of Askelon;
Lest the daughters of the Philistines rejoice,
Lest the daughters of the uncircumcised triumph.
Ye mountains of Gilboa,
Let there be no dew nor rain upon you, neither fields of offerings,
For there the shield of the mighty was vainly cast away,
The shield of Saul, not anointed with oil,
From the blood of the slain, from the fat of the mighty,
The bow of Jonathan turned not back,
And the sword of Saul returned not empty.
Saul and Jonathan were lovely and pleasant in their lives,
And in their death they were not divided;
They were swifter than eagles,
They were stronger than lions.
Ye daughters of Israel, weep over Saul,
Who clothed you in scarlet delicately,
Who put ornaments of gold upon your apparel.
How are the mighty fallen in the midst of the battle!
Jonathan is slain upon thy high places.
I am distressed for thee, my brother Jonathan:
Very pleasant hast thou been unto me:
Thy love to me was wonderful,
Passing the love of woman,
How are the mighty fallen, and the weapons of war perished!"
(2 Sam. 1 : 19-27.)

John Milton, the Prince of Poets, once said, "There are no songs comparable to the songs of Zion." Also, he said, in speaking of the Psalms: "Not in their divine argument alone, but in the very critical art of composition, they may be easily made appear over all the kinds of lyric poesy to be incomparable."

Dr. Johnson, the great critic, once remarked of Joseph Addison: "Whoever wishes to attain an English style, familiar but not coarse, and elegant but not ostentatious, must give his days and nights to the volumes of Addison." He (Addison) says: "Homer has innumerable flights that Virgil was not able to reach, and in the Old Testament we find several passages more elevated and sublime than any in Homer." And, also: "After perusing the Book of Psalms, let a judge of the beauties of poetry read a literal translation of Horace or Pindar, and he will find in these two last such an absurdity and confusion of style, with such a comparative poverty of imagination, as will make him sensible of the vast superiority of the Scripture style."

Baron Humboldt once referring to the 104th Psalm, said: "We are astonished to find in a lyrical poem of such a limited compass the whole universe—the heavens and the earth—sketched with a few bold touches. This contrast and generalization in the conception of natural phenomena, and the retrospection of an omnipresent, invisible Power, which can renew the earth or crumble it to dust, constitutes a solemn and exalted form of poetic creation."

HISTORY.

Sir Isaac Newton once said: "I find more sure marks of authenticity in the Bible than in any profane history whatever."

The Bible contains the most ancient history of any book in the world. It reaches centuries beyond Josephus, Xenophon, and Herodotus, clear back to the dawn of creation. The confirmations that are being made of the accuracy of its statements, by archæological discoveries are indeed extraordinary. It would seem that almost every turn of the spade is bringing to light some corroboration of scriptural statement. The cuneiform inscriptions and tablets of Nineveh and Babylon; the hieroglyphics of Luxor and Karnak; the "Rosetta" stone; the "Moabite" stone; the "Siloam" inscription; the black monolith of Shalmaneser; etc., etc.—these all speak from out the dust of the centuries in corroboration of the Scriptural record. These testimonies are playing havoc with the ancient histories written by men. Someone has said: "Already over two thousand mistakes have been found in the best ancient history man ever wrote." Not one mistake, however, has been proved against the Bible.

The Babylonian history recorded in Genesis terminates with the fourteenth chapter. The remaining portion has a Syrian and Egyptian setting.

The explorations made at Nineveh by Sir A. H. Layard have brought to light the ruined library of the ancient city which lay buried under the mounds of Konyunjik. The three expeditions conducted by

Mr. George Smith, and the later ones of Mr. Hormuzd Rassam have added very largely to the stock of tablets from Konyunjik.

Prof. Sayce tells us "Although only one of the many libraries which now lie buried beneath the ground in Babylon and Assyria has, as yet, been at all adequately explored, the amount of Assyrian literature at the disposal of the student is already greater than that contained in the whole of the Old Testament."

Nearly every historical statement in the first fourteen chapters of Genesis has been verified by the cuneiform inscriptions already exhumed. The story of creation; the fall of man; the deluge; the story of Babel; the dispersion of mankind; Nimrod; Abraham, Sarah and Lot; the campaign of Chedor-Laomer; etc., etc.; are told and described on the tablets of this one library.

The Egyptologist, also, is having the same kind of experience. He has, in his research, fully verified the Scriptural story of Joseph. M. Naville has corroborated the Bible date of the Exodus, and proved the personality of the Pharaoh of the oppression, by his excavations at Tel-el-Meokhuta. Prof. Sayce says that M. Naville has not only discovered the ruins of Pithon or Succoth, one of the Treasure cities of Joseph's time, but, "Has even discovered the treasure-chambers themselves. They are very strongly constructed, and divided by brick partitions from eight to ten feet thick, the bricks being sun-baked, and made some with and some without straw. In these strawless bricks we may see the work of the oppressed people when the order came: 'Thus saith Pharaoh, I will not give you straw.'"

Nearly three hundred historical statements of the Bible have been corroborated by the labors of Egyptologists up to the present time.

With regard to Assyrian history, Prof. Sayce has made a list of seventy-seven events, running from B.C. 1130 to B.C. 513, that the archæologists have deciphered from the records they have exhumed, all of which agree substantially with the record made in the Scriptures of the same events.

These verifications prove to a demonstration that the historical record of the Bible was given by Almighty God.

Dr. W. C. Prime, a life-long student of Egyptology has expressed himself concerning this matter in the following explicit and emphatic manner, in the New York Observer:

"To students of history it is impossible to deny the commanding position occupied by the Hebrew books, among the literature of the past. Their truthfulness compared with that of secular histories, is little less than miraculous. No extant history, outside of the collection known as the Bible, ancient or modern, has failed to show the tendency of the human historian to error if not to wilful falsification. There has never yet been published a history of the United States or of England or of France, a history of our own Civil War, or of any war in Europe, a history of any period or any series of events, which has not been demonstrated to contain mistakes, and misrepresentations. The father of history, Herodotus, prepared with great labor a history of ancient Egypt. Modern exploration, bringing to light the buried art and the buried men of ancient Egypt, has ascertained that in many respects he was misinformed. It became necessary to have an annotated Herodotus, in which his errors are corrected by the indisputable evidence of the monuments. The work of the Hebrew Moses deals extensively with Egyptian history, politics, manners and customs, in a period nearly forty centuries ago. It has not become necessary to make a solitary note on the margin of this history to say that Moses was mistaken. Wherever discovered Egyptian remains have given us information concerning any subject touched by the books of Moses, there the invariable rule has been the confirmation, in the minutest particulars, of the accuracy of the Hebrew historian. We have no need of any annotation to correct one error of Moses.

Now if this were true of Herodotus, or of Macaulay, or of any historian concerning whose work no one had ever suggested supernatural inspiration, that historian would rank in the world of literature as immeasurably above all other authors. He would unquestionably stand as the most admired, respected, and honored writer known to the human race. When we consider the proneness of men to err, the moral impossibility of any man's avoiding mistake even in the common concerns of life, it may be considered very certain that if, in ordinary literature, there were such a historian, of whom no one could say he had committed an error in any line he had written, the critic, the intelligent world, every sensible reader of his work would unhesitatingly say: "This work is miraculous."

I am not dealing with the question of Inspiration. I am discussing only the position of Moses in the rank of historians. It is a literary, not a religious question. I am asking you to divest yourself of any conscious or unconscious prejudice against claims of supernaturalism, and to consider the wonderful supremacy of this author over all other authors; a supremacy which demonstrates that in his intellectual labors Truth occupied a controlling power over mind and pen which it has never occupied in the mind of any one in the long catalogue of secular historians, ancient or modern.

I have not space to review those recent discoveries in Egypt which, to the critics who profess to have no faith in Moses (or even in a Moses), have again so startlingly demonstrated his accurate knowledge of Asiatic as well as Egyptian conditions, in and before his time, and the folly and falsehood of their intuitive conclusions. No point has been more clear to them than that Melchisedek, King of Salem and Priest of the Most High God, was a fancy of ages long after the supposed date of Moses, and not a historical personage. This same criticism, based wholly on intuition without information, has also taught the absolute impossibility of any such social, political and literary conditions, contemporary with Abraham, as are assumed and mentioned by Moses.

The Tel-el-Amarna discoveries include a large amount of diplomatic and personal correspondence between the Egyptian Pharaohs and Asiatic Kings. They demonstrate a high civilization, a widespread knowledge of Asiatic languages and literature, close relations of correspondence in Asiatic letters, and a political condition identical with that recognized by Moses and discredited by modern critical imaginations. Most interesting among these are letters from a king of Jerusalem somewhere near B.C. 1400 or 1500, a successor of Melchisedek, who, in the ancient style of princes, describes himself and his independent royalty, as derived from God only, in the terms used by Moses, and extended by later sacred writers. He says that no father or mother placed him in his kingship, no king of Egypt made him king, only the oracle of the Mighty King, the God of Jerusalem, Uru-salem, City of Peace. Moses in mentioning Melchisedek, uses an accurate description.

The Hebrew historian knew perfectly well the tenure of royalty in the kingdom of Jerusalem. His words are correct. A voice out of the tomb of thirty centuries confirms the historical accuracy of Moses and demolishes the whole system of Biblical criticisms, which has taught that this portion of the Book of Genesis was "impossible of truth," a pure imagination.

Will it stay demolished? Not at all. It will stand in pulpits, sit in chairs of lecturing, and all who do not want to believe in Moses will admire the self-sufficient folly of teachers who say: "We don't believe in Moses because we don't believe in him."

Trustworthy literature of the covenant with Noah and with Abraham has been preserved to us in inscriptions, traditions and memoirs which no respectable critic dare deny. The records of Abraham, the rite of circumcision, the slaughter of Hamor and of the men of Shechem, the escape from Egypt and the renewal of the covenant rite at Gilgal, stand to-day perfectly intact, despite all criticism. These are marvels of history. Add the sacramental passover and the daily sacrifice and we have the essence of the first six books of the Old Covenant. These witnesses are contained in monuments and certified by institutions and by the Hebrew history for more than two thousand years. Mr. Pinches tells us from the early inscriptions that the Chinese, who migrated from Chaldea in the twenty-third century B.C., have traditions of *Creation, of Paradise, the Tree of Knowledge, the temptation by the serpent, the fall of man, the curse upon him, ideas of satan and angels, traditions of the deluge, and the dispersion of mankind.*

PHILOSOPHY.

The philosophy of the Bible is not equaled by anything written by Aristotle, Plato, Socrates, Newton, Locke, Hegel or Bacon. Sir Isaac Newton said: "I account the Scriptures of God to be the most sublime philosophy."

Coleridge said: "The Bible finds me at greater depths of my being than any other book."

Rousseau, infidel though he was, once wrote—

"Peruse the works of our philosophers, with all their pomp of diction, how mean, how contemptible are they compared with the Scriptures."

Carlyle was very fond of the Bible. Once, after reading it at length, he exclaimed, "A noble Book! All men's Book!" He was passionately fond of Job, which is, without doubt, the most remarkable philosophical treatise in the world. His literary friends knew of this passion, and oftentimes, at the club, they would ask him to read aloud the first chapter of the book. Directly after beginning he would invariably become so lost to all things else, that he would not cease to read until the last word of the entire book was pronounced, the while those present were laughing at him, or talking about other matters.

BIOGRAPHY.

The biographies of the Bible are strikingly unique. The men of the Scriptures are real, natural, true-to-life men. Not so other biographical characters. When men write of their friends they say all the good things they can of them, and usually touch up their statements with glowing colors, and always omit mention of anything disparagingly. So true is this, that the minister, in preaching a funeral sermon, must not mention any bad traits or weaknesses belonging to the character and life of the deceased.

When God gave the record of the lives and doings of the men of old—His friends, He made it according to the facts in the case. He tells us of Noah's drunkenness; Abraham's lying; the rascalities of

Jacob; the dissembling of Moses; how King David committed adultery and murder; and all about the lying and profanity of Peter. The men of the Bible are neighbors of ours. This is true of no biography that any man ever wrote of his friends, and is a demonstration of the Divine authorship of the Book.

What drama did Shakespeare write that will at all compare with Saul and the witch of Endor? or David and Absalom? or, Elijah, Ahab and Jezebel? or a score more, contained in the Bible, that might be mentioned?

The imagery of the Bible is far more skillfully drawn, and artistically colored, than anything that man or woman ever did.

The character drawing of the Bible is true to life, and the best work of Dickens and Thackeray is not to be mentioned by comparison.

Is it not true that the best and most gifted authors are those who have used the Bible most? Hundreds of books in our libraries would not have outlived those who wrote them, but for the style, knowledge and enthusiasm the authors borrowed from the Bible, and incorporated into their pages. Indeed, the Bible has had more to do with imparting life and longevity to other books, than any other reason that can be named. What would the world's literature be to-day, if there had been no Bible? It has lifted literature to its present exalted position, and decorated it with a wealth of beauty to which it otherwise must have forevermore remained a stranger. We know, therefore, from these and other reasons, that the Bible, as a literary work, stands at the head of the list, and is, by comparison, without doubt, the Book of books.

CHAPTER VI.

THE BIBLE AND SCIENCE.

Theology is man's knowledge of God's word systematized and classified. Science is man's knowledge of God's works, systematized and classified. Man's knowledge is necessarily limited and imperfect. Therefore, theology and science are oftentimes in conflict, and must ever be; but, between God's word and works, there is perfect harmony.

It is quite natural for human minds to discredit the supernatural. Most of the " Higher Critics " do this in their views of inspiration. The miraculous is not necessarily unscientific, it is not the setting aside or overriding of laws. A miracle is simply God doing something according to certain laws of which we know nothing. To illustrate: If I had said, twenty years ago, I talked with a man the other day one hundred miles away, just as though he were ten feet distant from me, it would have been called a miracle, and why? Simply because there was then no law of acoustics known, by which the human voice could be transmitted one hundred miles; but, within these twenty years, such a law has been discovered, and our voices may be heard by our friends one hundred, or one thousand miles away, and it is not called a miracle. I doubt not there are ten thousand laws operating in the universe of which man knows nothing, to every one concerning which he may truthfully say: I know the method by which it operates.

The axioms of science are but few. It not infrequently happens that that which has been classified among the scientific certainties, has been displaced, as a result of subsequent research and discovery. Man is predisposed in favor of his own conjectures. We have a striking illustration of this in the "Progressive Evolution" theory of Charles Darwin, which so many accepted without hesitation, but which he, with humiliation, was afterwards obliged to greatly modify.

When one, standing amidst scientific discoveries and deductions, says, "Here, at least, we have an unmovable footing: we stand among the certainties;" the sound of his words may be pleasant to his ears, and the thought may minister to his vanity; but to thoughtful and reverent minds there is very much of nonsense in his utterances.

A skeptical young man once flippantly inquired of a devout old farmer, "Don't you know that science has disproved the Bible?" "What science? I haven't read the morning papers today," was the quick reply.

The Bible is not a text-book for the schools, upon the physical sciences; but, it has not a little to say about the works of God, and what it does say, is said accurately and well, and can always be relied upon.

Lieutenant Maury, than whom none stood higher in his department of science, once said: "In my investigation of natural science, I have always found that whenever I can meet with anything in the Bible on any subject, it always affords me a fine platform on which to stand, and a round in the ladder by which I could safely ascend."

Prof. Dana once said: "The grand old Book of God still stands, and this old earth, the more its leaves are turned over and pondered, the more it will sustain and illustrate the Sacred Word."

Friedrich H. A. Von Humboldt said: "As descriptions of nature, the writings of the Old Testament are a faithful reflection of the character of the country in which they were composed, of the alternations of barrenness and fruitfulness, and of the Alpine forests by which Palestine was characterized. They describe, in their regular succession, the relations of the climate, the manners of this people of herdsmen, and their hereditary aversion to agricultural pursuits."

In 1831, "The British Association for the Advancement of Science" was established by Sir David Brewster and others, and, while all its members are not necessarily scientists, yet an overwhelming majority of them are the highest scientists in the world. This association in 1865, drew up a paper which was signed by six hundred and seventeen members, twenty only of whom were not recognized men of science, setting forth their views on the relations between science and religion, and how these relations should be treated. This important and remarkable document is accessible to anyone in the

Bodleian Library in Oxford, England, and is as follows:

"We, the undersigned students of the natural sciences, desire to express our sincere regret that researches into scientific truth are perverted by some, in our times, into occasions for casting doubt upon the truth and authenticity of the Holy Scriptures.

"We conceive that it is impossible for the Word of God, as written in the book of Nature, and God's Word written in the Holy Scripture, to contradict one another, however much they may appear to differ.

"We are not forgetful that physical science is not complete, but is only in a condition of progress, and that at present our finite reason enables us only to see as through a glass darkly; and we confidently believe that a time will come when the two records will be seen to agree in every particular.

"We cannot but deplore that natural science should be looked upon with suspicion by many who do not make a study of it, merely on account of the unadvised manner in which some are placing it in opposition to Holy Writ.

"We believe it is the duty of every scientific student to investigate Nature simply for the purpose of elucidating truth, and that, if he finds that some of his results appear to be in contradiction to the written Word, or rather to his own interpretation of it, which may be erroneous, he should not presumptuously affirm that his own conclusions must be right, and the statements of Scripture wrong. Rather leave the two side by side till it shall please God to allow us to see the manner in which they may be reconciled; and instead of insisting upon the seeming differences between Science and the Scriptures, it would be as well to rest in faith upon the points in which they agree."

Let us notice a few cases, by way of illustrating the truth of what these distinguished scientists have said.

Once, in a "Drawing Room," in the late Earl of Shaftesbury's home, the subject under consideration was the first chapter of Genesis. A distinguished Bible scholar was conducting the study. He called attention to the fact that in this account of creation, the order of genera is scientifically correct. Heaven, earth, water, light, firmament, grass, herb, tree, heavenly bodies, fish, moving things (amphibia), fowls, creeping things, cattle and man. The possible permutations of fifteen numerals approximates an almost incomprehensible number, *i. e.* 1,307,674,368,000. In order to show how impossible it would be for the writer of this chapter to get these events correct in their order, if he wrote only as a man, he took a slip of paper, and on it he wrote fifteen numbers, from one to fifteen inclusive. Under each one of these numbers he wrote a letter of the English alphabet, choosing the first fifteen, but not writing them in their regular order, but as confusedly as he could. Then he took fifteen slips of paper, and on each one wrote a number, the fifteen agreeing with the fifteen on his slip. Then he passed these slips to fifteen different persons, one to each, and then asked them as he called the numbers, one by one, for the persons having the slips to write the letters he had written on the slip before him. One can see, at a glance, that these fifteen persons could get the fifteen letters in the same order in which they were written on the slip held by the teacher, by the merest possible chance, if they were to live many years and did nothing else but try.

In the twenty-sixth chapter of Job and seventh verse we are told: " He stretcheth out the north over empty space." Astronomers who were skeptically inclined, turned their telescopes to the northward, and ransacking the heavens in that direction, could find no " empty space ;" and then, they would twit the Theologues, by saying: "Job knew nothing about the geography of the heavens. He had better left astronomical matters alone, and attended to the things nearer home with which he was better acquainted, his boils, for instance." Then the Theologues, instead of insisting that Job did know what he was talking about, undertook to parry the thrust by saying: " Job evidently referred to the north pole," feeling quite safe in making such a suggestion with seven or eight hundred miles of impenetrable ice-barrier intervening. Some years ago, the late Prof. Loomis, of Yale University, in speaking about this matter, told me that, " Recently, by the use of the largest telescope in the northern hemisphere, in the Naval Observatory, at Washington, a great vacuum, corresponding to the "empty space" of which Job wrote, has been discovered in the depths of the northern heavens." How did Job know of this?

"Joshua's Long Day" has been hooted at and decried by skeptics; and, too often Christian Ministers and teachers disbelieve the record of it, pass it by, or explain it away. On the basis of the publications of "The British Chronological Society," Prof. Totten, of Yale University, has "Corroborated by Eclipses," "Verified by Equinoxes," and "Proved by the Almanac" that the Scriptural account of the Long Day in Joshua, the tenth chapter, and the moving backward of the Shadow ten degrees on the "Dial of Ahaz" (Isa. 38 chap.) are scientifically correct, and this to a demonstration. (See "Joshua's Long Day," by C. A. L. Totten, M.A.)

Herodotus tells us of certain records, wholly independent of the Hebrew account, shown him by priests while in Egypt, containing an account of a "Long Day," which agreed with the Scriptural narrative.

The Chinese, also, have an entirely independent account of a "Long Day" agreeing with the record in the tenth chapter of Joshua, which occurred in the reign of Yeo, who was contemporary with Joshua.

Jonah and the Whale is stock in trade for the skeptic. He proves by two incontrovertible arguments that Jonah could not have been swallowed by a whale. First, there were no whales in the Mediterranean Sea; and second, a whale's gullet is not large enough to swallow a man whole. Both of these arguments are untrue. Whales of the species called by Cuvier the *Rorqual Mediterranensis*, have been found in this sea, and even as distinguished authority as Thomas Beale observes in speaking of the spermaceti whale, that "the throat is capacious enough to give passage to the body of a man." We mention these two facts simply to show how reckless and unscientific some of our skeptical friends are in discussing biblical questions. Let me emphasize the fact, for we are all apt to be careless readers of the Bible, that the word whale is not once used in the Book of Jonah. This is true, as well of the English as of the Hebrew. The latter uses *dag gathol*, and the former *great fish*. Unfortunately our translators have rendered Kētos, of the New Testament, whale, but certainly without good reasons, for according to the best Greek scholars, Kētos means any sea monster or huge fish, such as a seal, shark, tunny, or whale; thus the term being indefinite, sea monster would be more correct than whale. It is now generally agreed that the fish in question must have been a shark. The shark is found in all seas; these fish often swallow very large animals, such as cattle and even horses. Not only that, but they often throw up whole and alive the prey they have swallowed. Any reader interested in this subject will find numerous and interesting instances of sharks swallowing very large objects, such as men, cattle, horses, etc., in the commentaries of Pusey and Keil, and also in the article "Whale," in Smith's *Bible Dictionary* or *M'Clintock and Strong's Cyclopedia.*

I once saw a marine monster off the Island of Cyprus, quite large enough to swallow an ordinary sized man.

I also once saw a whale eighty-four feet long and twenty-six feet in diameter at the largest part of his body. Surely the God who made such a monster, could easily enough enlarge his throat, if necessary, sufficiently to make it easy for him to swallow a man.

But recently the remains of a whale were discovered upon the coast of Norway, with a throat so large that he could have swallowed a man on horseback, horse and all.

Notwithstanding all these facts, skeptics will still make "Jonah and the whale" do duty, until the end of time.

Messrs. Charles Scribner's Sons, of New York, have recently published a deeply interesting volume. It is the last work of the late Rev. Austin Phelps, D.D., LL.D., who was for many years the President of Andover Theological Seminary, and the author of many learned treatises. This work, which is entitled *My Note Book*, was prepared just before the great scholar's death. "If I can only live," he wrote to a friend, "till this book is done, I shall be content to go." He did live to finish it, and the last letter he received was one from the publishers acknowledging the receipt of the manuscript. His famous daughter, Mrs. Elizabeth Stuart P. Ward, has read the proofs, and added an introduction after his death, but found no necessity for making any changes in the book. As its name implies, the volume is fragmentary, containing the jottings and stray thoughts of years, but the fragments are gems of rare value, all the more precious because they are the last we shall ever have from the pen which has written so much and so well. Among "the fragments" are the following observations, which, coming, as they do from so learned a man, are entitled to the attention of students of prophecy.

A service of very peculiar nature and not generally known, connects the books of our faith with the researches of astronomical science. It is well understood by experts in astronomy that a certain complicated cycle which should harmonize certain intricate revolutions of the solar system, has been sought for, for centuries. At last, it was until recently, given up as being beyond the reach of human discovery. But within a few years, an eminent Swiss astronomer professes to have found the long-sought marvel of astronomical science. His researches have been submitted to three distinguished astronomers of the "Royal Academy of Sciences" in Paris. By them it has been pronounced accurate and of practical value.

The interesting fact about this astronomical discovery is that the discoverer was first led to suspect the existence of the cycle, by a study of the symbolical prophecies of Daniel. It is well known that the majority of the interpreters have found in those prophecies a period of 2300 solar years, as the measurement in the prophetic visions, of the time which should elapse between the age of Daniel and the end of the so-called *Times of the Gentiles*. The Swiss astronomer—M. de Cheseaux, by name—is a devout believer in the Scriptures. In reading the symbolical predictions of Daniel, it occurred to him as a hypothesis that this period of twenty-three centuries might be the cycle so long despaired of by experts in astronomical science. On further investigation, by astronomical methods, he found that it was even so. The discovery led to that of other cycles, all involved in the prophetic computations, and by means of which he was able to solve between thirty and forty astronomical and geographical problems.

He suggests, plausibly, to say the least, the inquiry, "How happened it that a Hebrew prophet, twenty-three centuries in advance of scientific discovery, used that occult cycle in his timing of coming events in the far distant future?" If he had conversed with the most eminent astronomers of his age, he could not have learned it from them. They knew nothing of its existence. If he had been, himself, the most accomplished scientist of the century, he could not have discovered it. There were no astronomical instruments in existence by which the requisite observations could have been made. The famed astrology of Chaldæa of which he may have known something, knew nothing of it. For twenty-three centuries that ignorance of the learned world has continued, notwithstanding the immense advances in astronomical knowledge, and in the improvement of the instruments of the observatory. Yet all the while the mysterious and unknown cycle lay embedded in the symbolic prophecies of the Hebrew seer. How happened that? Not one only, but a system of co-ordinate cycles was made the groundwork of prophetic computations.

How came that about? The theory of the discoverer is, that a foreordained synchronism exists between the movements of the solar system and the developments of human history. The chronologies of the two are one. The mind which contrived the one foreordained the other. The clock-work of the material heavens and the clock-work of the history of man have been created and wound up by the same Being. So reasons the devout astronomer. Of course none but proficients in astronomical researches and proficients in the interpretation of symbolic prophecy can pronounce independently upon the value of the discoveries. But the conditions attending their announcement entitle them to the consideration of Biblical scholars. They place the hallowed books of our religion in very interesting relation to human science.—*The Christian Herald.*

In the lists of animals there occur nine in Deuteronomy which do not appear in Leviticus. Of these, five or six at least, probably more, are creatures which do not, and never could have, lived in the rich valley of the Nile, or in wooded and hilly Palestine. They are all the inhabitants of desert open plains, or of bare, rocky heights. They are not named in Leviticus, because immediately after the Exodus these antelopes and desert denizens were strange to the Israelites. But after thirty-nine years had been passed in their haunts, they must have been familiar with them all. Is it conceivable that any writer of the later monarchy should have inserted in his catalogue animals which he could never have seen or known but by report?

Harvey discovered the law of the circulation of blood, and, although he demonstrated it by uncovering the heart of a live cat so that its action could be seen, yet not one scientific man in one hundred in his day would believe it. And yet this law is plainly stated in Eccl. 12 : 6.

Jesus said, that when He would return a second time to earth, it would be "Even" at one point, "Midnight" at another, "Cock-crowing" at another, and "Morning" at another (see Mark 13 : 35). In fact He said the world was round. And yet, it was thirteen hundred years before a man saw it, and when he did, he was persecuted most unpityingly by the scientific men of his day for believing what he saw.

In these and other cases that might be cited, we see the truth of what Sir John Herschel once said, viz.: "All human discoveries seem to be made only for the purpose of confirming more and more strongly, the truths contained in the Sacred Scriptures."

CHAPTER VII.

THE ETHICS OF THE BIBLE.

Our objecting friend will tell us that the writings of Confucius, Zoroaster and the old Pagan Philosophers are, ethically considered, as good, if not better, than the Bible. It is no doubt true that these men had much light; and that they had a pretty correct conception of a very great deal of ethical truth. From whence did they get their light and knowledge? I reply, From the Bible. Our friend don't know two things, viz.: First, that every principle of ethical truth known to the world to-day may be found, at least in germ form, in the Pentateuchal books and the book of Job; and, Second, that these books are the oldest in the world, and were written centuries before these ancient writers were born. We know that they were, to some extent, familiar with the Hebrew Bible. By these and other facts we know that they borrowed much of what they wrote from the Bible.

There used to go about the country a notorious and blatant infidel; and enemies of righteousness gave him tens of thousands of dollars to hear him revile the Bible. He does not go around any more. The people got tired of paying him their dollars, and as that was the only thing he was after, except notoriety, he remains at home now the most of his time. In one of his assaults upon the Bible, he would pick up a copy of the volume, and after reading a few verses from it, stop abruptly, and, closing the book, throw it down with a slam, and then say, "I beg the pardon of this audience; I don't dare to insult your intelligence and decency by reading further." And then every man present, living a licentious life, would applaud to the echo.

It is true there are things in the Bible I would not read to a congregation of men and women. But does that fact prove the book to be immoral and untrue? Ought it on that account to be burned? Go into any physician's office and you will find books, the contents of which no one would think of reading to an audience composed of both sexes. And why? Because they treat of the pathology and therapeutics of human diseases. Are these books necessarily immoral? Ought they to be burned on this account? The Bible treats of the pathology and therapeutics of moral diseases and infirmities, that are immeasurably more dreadful and awful than physical and mental disorders. What wonder, therefore, that it contains statements that it would be improper to read to a mixed congregation. And it was never intended they should be.

A thoroughly dishonest trick of infidel scoffers is to call Germany, England and the United States Christian Nations; and then pointing to the many diabolical things done by citizens of these nations, who hate the Bible, hold the Bible responsible for them. These men know that all lovers of the Bible are opposed to the slave trade, the opium and liquor traffics, polygamy and the licensing of all forms of evil, bitterly, uncompromisingly and eternally opposed to these and all other iniquitous things; and are always to be found in the fore-front of the battle for the right as against the wrong. The trouble in this matter lies in the assumption that these are Christian Nations. The majority rules, and as the majority do not love the Bible, or walk, act and live according to its precepts and commandments, these immoralities and abominations are permitted and legalized: but the enemies, and not the friends, of the Bible, are responsible.

In what land under the sun is woman, in any sense, the companion and equal of man, save in those where the Bible is an open Book? In what country of the earth are eleemosynary institutions to be found, save where the Bible is freely read and preached? The Bible has put a school-house on every hill-top, and built a university, college, seminary or academy in almost every county in so-called Christian lands. Nine-tenths of educational institutions were founded, as they are controlled, by those who love the Bible. These institutions are not to be found in countries where the Bible is not honored and exalted. The Bible has gone before the white wings of commerce upon all seas; and has been in the fore-front of exploration and discovery of all known lands. Its principles of equity and justice are fundamental, in the common law. It is the bed-rock foundation of the highest and best forms of civilization, and is the World's Magna

Charta of civil liberty. It has broken the shackles of the slave. It has comfort for the sorrowing, and hope for the despairing. It has put vice under bonds to keep the peace, and put highest premium upon honesty, virtue and holiness. The late Earl of Shaftesbury once said: "One city missionary is as effective in guarding the peace of a community as one hundred policemen." It is the best and most satisfactory police power in the world.

I once read of a man who was traveling in the wilds of Kentucky many years ago. He had considerable money with him. He also was well armed. One night he was obliged to stop at a double log cabin in an out-of-the-way place. There were a number of men about, backwoodsmen, and, to the eye of this man, pretty rough looking. The traveler retired early, but not to sleep. He put his money under the bed, and his pistols under the pillow. In about an hour after retiring, he was startled by the barking of dogs and the noise of someone entering the cabin. He got his pistols and sat up in bed, and looking through a crack into the other room, saw a man he had not before seen, standing a gun in a corner of the room. The other men sat before the fire. The new arrival joined them. They spent some time in earnest conversation. The traveler could not hear what they said, but felt sure they were plotting to rob, or possibly kill him. Presently the late-comer, who seemed to be the oldest, arose and stepping to the side of the room, took from a shelf a copy of the Bible. He read a chapter aloud. When through, they all knelt while he offered prayer. The traveler at once dismissed his fears, put his pistols away, and, lying down, slept peacefully until the morning, and all because there was a Bible in the house, and the rough backwoodsmen living there loved it, and tried to be guided and governed by its teachings.

Where, in the wide world, are there to be found maxims, adages and rules for conduct, at all comparable to those in the Proverbs and Ecclesiastes, and the Sermon on the Mount, and the Thirteenth Chapter of First Corinthians? We have books written by Æsop, Macchiavelli, Dr. Franklin, John Stuart Mill, Dr. John G. Holland, and a host of other gifted writers, on the laws of living and rules of conduct, books that contain a vast amount of wisdom, often beautifully and forcibly stated. But compare them with the maxims of Solomon, and it will not take one, competent to judge, a great while to see that they are of a very inferior order. A student came into the study of Dr. Wayland, when he was President of Brown University, one day, and said: "Dr. Wayland, I have been reading the Proverbs of Solomon, and I don't think they amount to much; I believe I can write better ones myself." "Well," said the doctor, "Suppose you take two weeks and write half a dozen, and, when done, bring them to me. I think I would like to see them." The student said he would, and withdrew. The two weeks passed, but he did not report. The wise old Doctor had not forgotten, and sent for him.

When he entered the President's office, Dr. Wayland inquired: "How about those maxims you were going to write for me?" "Well!" responded the student, "I haven't succeeded. I thought it would be an easy thing to do, those in the Bible seemed so simple and common-place; but the more I tried, the more I found that I couldn't do it, and, after boasting as I did, I was ashamed to come to you and acknowledge my failure."

Prof. Huxley is about the last man one would expect to say anything favorably of the Bible; yet in an article, published in the Contemporary Review, Dec. 1870, from his pen, he says this: "Take the Bible as a whole; make the severest deductions which fair criticisms can dictate for shortcomings and positive errors; eliminate, as a sensible teacher would do, if left to himself, all that it is not desirable for a child to occupy himself with; and there still remains in this old literature a vast residuum of moral beauty and grandeur. And then consider the great historical fact that, for three centuries, this book has been woven into the life of all that is best and noblest in English history; that it has become the national epic of Britain, and is familiar to noble and simple, from John o' Groat's house to Land's End, as Dante and Tasso were once to the Italians."

Rousseau, infidel though he was, once said: "If all men were perfect Christians, individuals would do their duty; the people would be obedient to the laws, governors would be just, and magistrates incorrupt."

Edmund Burke once said: "A religious education is the cheap defense of nations." And for himself he said: "I have read the Bible morning, noon and night, and have ever since been the happier and better man for such reading."

Lord Bacon said: "There never was found, in any age of the world, either religion or law that did so highly exalt the public good as the Bible."

John Locke, the illustrious metaphysician, said: "In morality there are books enough written both by ancient and modern philosophers, but the morality of the Gospel doth so exceed them all, that to give a man a full knowledge of true morality, I shall send him to no other book than the New Testament."

Cowper wrote:

> Now tell me, dignified and sapient sir,
> My man of morals, nurtured in the shad
> Of Academus, is this false or true?
> Is Christ the abler teacher, or the schools?
> If Christ, then why resort at every turn
> To Athens, or to Rome, for wisdom short
> Of man's occasions, when in him reside
> Grace, knowledge, comfort, an unfathomed store?

Benj. Franklin, on one occasion, remarked: "A Bible and a newspaper in every house, a good school in every district, all studied and appreciated as they merit, are the principal support of virtue, morality, and civil liberty."

During his last illness, General Andrew Jackson pointed to the family Bible and said to a friend: "That Book, sir, is the rock on which our republic rests."

Wm. H. Seward, one of America's most able and distinguished statesmen, said, on one occasion: "The whole hope of human progress is suspended on the ever-growing influence of the Bible." At another time he remarked: "I do not believe human society, including not merely a few persons in any state, but whole masses of men, ever has attained, or can ever attain, a high state of intelligence, virtue, security, liberty, or happiness, without the Holy Scriptures."

The distinguished French statesman De Tocqueville once wrote: "Bible Christianity is the companion of liberty in all its conflicts, the cradle of its infancy, and the divine source of its claims."

In the early part of the year 1891, Hon. W. E. Gladstone said to Dr. T. DeWitt Talmage: "The older I grow, the more confirmed I am in my faith in religion. Sir," said he, with flashing eye and uplifted hand, "talk about the questions of the day, there is but one question, and that is the Gospel. That can and will correct everything. I am glad to say that about all the men at the top in Great Britain are Christians. Why, sir," he said, "I have been in public position fifty-eight years, and forty-seven years in the Cabinet of the British Government, and during those forty-seven years I have been associated with sixty of the master minds of the century, and all but five of the sixty were Christians."

Abraham Lincoln said: "In regard to the Great Book, I have only to say, it is the best gift which God has given to man. All the good from the Saviour of the world is communicated through this Book.

But for this Book, we could not know right from wrong. All those things desirable to man are contained in it."

General Grant said: "Hold fast to the Bible as the sheet-anchor of your liberties, write its precepts in your hearts, and practice them in your lives. To the influence of this Book are we indebted for all the progress made in true civilization; and to this must we look as our guide in the future."

England's noble and best Queen, Victoria, was once asked, by an African Prince, who visited her court on an embassy, what was the secret of England's greatness. The Queen handed him a beautifully bound copy of the Bible, and said: "Tell the Prince that this is the secret of England's greatness."

The following beautiful poem was written by the good Quaker John G. Whittier:

> O lady fair, these silks of mine
> Are beautiful and rare,
> The richest web of the India loom,
> Which beauty's queen might wear;
> And my pearls are pure as thy own fair neck,
> With whose radiant light they vie:
> I have brought them with me a weary way:
> Will my gentle lady buy?
>
> And the lady smiled on the worn old man,
> Through the dark and clustering curls
> Which veiled her brow as she bent to view
> His silks and glittering pearls;
> And she placed the price in the old man's hand,
> And lightly turned away;
> But she paused at the wanderer's call,—
> My gentle lady, stay!

O lady fair, I have yet a gem
Which a purer luster flings
Than the diamond flash of the jeweled crown
On the lofty brow of Kings,—
A wonderful pearl of exceeding price,
Whose virtues shall not decay,
Whose light shall be as a spell to thee,
And a blessing on thy way.

The lady glanced at the mirroring steel
Where her form of grace was seen,
Where her eyes shone clear and her dark locks waved
Their clasping pearls between.
"Bring forth thy pearl of exceeding worth,
Thou traveler gray and old,
And name the price of thy precious gem
And my page shall count the gold."

The cloud went off from the pilgrim's brow,
As a small and meager book,
Uncased with gold or gem of cost
From his folding robe he took!
"Here, lady fair, is the pearl of price,
May it prove as such to thee!
Nay—keep thy gold—I ask it not,
For the Word of God is free!"

The hoary traveler went his way,
But the gift he left behind
Hath had its pure and perfect work
On the high born maiden's mind.
And she hath turned from the pride of sin
To the lowliness of truth,
And given her human heart to God
In its beautiful hour of youth.

And she hath left the gray old halls,
Where an evil faith hath power,
The courtly knights of her father's train,
And the maidens of her bower;
And she hath gone to the Vaudois vales,
By lordly feet untrod,
Where the poor and needy of earth are rich
In the perfect love of God.

CHAPTER VIII.

PROPHECIES OF THE BIBLE.

Men have in all ages, and by all possible means, endeavored in vain to unlock the future. God only knows its mysteries. If there were no other reason for believing that the Bible has God for its Author, its prophetic utterances, that we know have been fulfilled, should dissipate all doubts.

I have counted more than one hundred and fifty distinct prophecies concerning Jesus Christ, found in nearly every Old Testament book, written from four hundred to fifteen hundred years before He was born, all of which were fulfilled in the most minute particular in His birth, life, passion, death, burial, resurrection and ascension. Glance at a few of these prophecies, and then consider the testimony of the Highest Critics as to their fulfillment.

BIRTH OF JESUS.

We are told in Gen. 3: 15, that Christ shall be the seed of the woman. In Gal. 4: 4, we find that it was even so. In Isa. 7: 14 it is declared "A virgin shall conceive and bear a son and shall call His name Immanuel." Matt. 1: 18–23 declares that this prophecy was fulfilled in the conception and birth of Jesus. So also does Luke 1: 26–35. It was prophesied by Micah that He would be born in Bethlehem Ephrathah, of Judah; and, according to Matt.

2:6; Luke 2:4; and John 7:42, it was even so. Gen. 12:3; 18:18; and 22:18 informs us that He was to be of the seed of Abraham. This is confirmed by the testimony of Matt. 1:1; John 8:56; and Acts 3:25. It was prophesied that Jesus would be of the tribe of Judah. And it came to pass. See Matt. 2:6; Heb. 7:14; and Rev. 5:5. It is declared in Isa. 11:1; 9:6, 7; Jer. 23:5, 6; Amos 9:11; and in several other places, that Jesus would be "Of the house and family of David." And so He was. See Matt. 1:1; Luke 1:69; 2:4; John 7:42; Acts 2:30; 13:22, 23; Rom. 1:3; 2 Tim. 2:8; and Rev. 22:16.

LIFE AND MINISTRY OF JESUS.

The heralding of Jesus, as prophesied in Isa. 40:3; and Mal. 3:1, was done by John the Baptist. See Mark 1:2; and Luke 3:3, 4. The flight of Joseph and Mary with the Child Jesus into Egypt was necessary that Hosea 11:1 might be fulfilled. Herod's slaughter of the children in Bethlehem was the fulfillment of Jer. 31:15, we are told, in Matt. 2:16. Jesus taking up His abode in Capernaum was according to the prophecy in Isa. 9:1, 2, so we are informed, in Matt. 8:16, 17. Jesus made no great ado in His work, but tried to keep His doings hid from public notice. See Matt. 12:15–17; which was according to Isa. 42;1–3. In Psa. 78:2, it is prophesied that He would teach in Parables. Matt. 13:34, 35 declares that this prophecy was fulfilled in His teaching. The people refused to receive His teaching. This was all foretold by Isaiah in chapter 6:10; and 53:1. See John 12:37-40. His riding into Jerusalem, as recorded in Matt. 21:1-5, was predicted in Zech. 9:9. The fleeing of the Disciples and leaving Him alone (Matt. 26:56) is just what Zechariah said would be done. See Zech. 13:7.

PASSION AND DEATH OF JESUS.

The passion of Jesus is foretold in Psa. 22:1-18; 31:13; 89:38-45; and particularly in the 53d chapter of Isaiah. Matt. 26:31; Luke 24:26; and Acts 8:32-35 inform us that in His sufferings these prophesies were fulfilled. We are told in John 3:14 that Jesus must be "Lifted up" even as typified in Numb. 21:9; and we know He was. The manner of His death is prophetically described in Psa. 22:16; and confirmed by John 20:25, 27. We are told that they who crucified Him cast lots for His vesture (See John 19:23, 24). This was foretold in Psa. 22:18. In John 19:33, we are told: "But when they came to Jesus and saw that He was dead already, they break not His legs." Psa. 34:20 says, "He keepeth all His bones, not one of them is broken."

BURIAL, RESURRECTION AND ASCENSION OF JESUS.

In Isaiah 53:9, we are told that "They made His grave with the wicked and rich in His death." And this is just what was done. See Matt. 27:57-60; Mark 15:43-46; Luke 23:50-53: John 19:38-42. In Acts 2:29-32 we are told explicitly that the resurrection of Jesus had taken place according to the prophecy of David, as recorded in Psalm 16:10. Jesus himself said: "Destroy this temple and in three days I will raise it up. * * * But he spake of the temple of his body." (John 2:19, 21). He here foretells the time He was to be in the grave, as well as the fact of His resurrection; which facts were typified by the swallowing of Jonah by the sea-monster, and his subsequent deliverance. See Matt. 12:40. After the death of Jesus the Scribes and Pharisees remembering what He had said—though the disciples seem to have forgotten it—about His resurrection, came to Pilate and besought him to take extra precautions against the thing foretold. See Matt. 27:62-66. But their vigilance and efforts to make void the prophecies and His own predictions, were futile.

In Psalm 110:1, it is said: "The Lord saith unto my Lord, sit thou at my right hand, until I make thine enemies thy footstool." Jesus Christ, in quoting this prophecy to the Pharisees, who sought to entangle Him in His words, left no doubt as to the particular person who was to be exalted. See Matt. 22:42-46. That He was so exalted, see Acts 1:9-11; 2:33; Rom. 8:33; Heb. 1:3; 2:9; 9:24; and Rev. 12:5. In Eph. 4:8-10, it is explicitly stated that the ascension of Jesus was in fulfillment of the prophecy in Psa. 68:18. Seven years after the ascension of our Lord, Stephen, "Being full of the Holy Ghost, looked up steadfastly into heaven, and saw the glory of God, and

Jesus, standing on the right hand of God, and said, Behold, I see the heavens opened, and the Son of man standing on the right hand of God." Acts 7: 55–56. It is the unfailing comfort of the Lord's people to know that, "If any man sin, we have an Advocate with the Father, Jesus Christ the righteous." 1 John 2: 1.

Among the last words spoken by Jesus to His Disciples were these: "And He said unto them, These are my words which I spake unto you while I was yet with you, how that all things must needs be fulfilled, which are written in the law of Moses, and the prophets, and the Psalms, concerning me. Then opened He their mind, that they might understand the Scriptures; and He said unto them, Thus it is written that the Christ should suffer, and rise again from the dead the third day; and that repentance and remission of sins should be preached in his name unto all nations, beginning from Jerusalem. Ye are witnesses of these things." Luke 24: 44–48.

The prophecies relating to the Christ are not the only ones which have been fulfilled. Consider those relating to the dispersion of the Jews, the destruction of Jerusalem and the wasting and desolation of Palestine, and you cannot help concluding that they are quite as extraordinary.

Take the prophecies of the building of Babylon, and the kingdom of Cyrus, uttered nearly one hundred and fifty years before anything was otherwise known of them. All fulfilled in exact detail. Dr. Newman, in his archæological researches among the ruins of Babylon, has declared, "I could take a competent engineer, if I had sufficient resources, and reconstruct Babylon, guided only by the prophecies uttered concerning it, long years before the first foundation stone was laid." We all know how fully the prophecies of the overthrow and destruction of Babylon were fulfilled. We know how all that was said prophetically of King Cyrus, one hundred and forty years before he was born, came to pass. Who among the wise men of earth can tell us who is to be born one hundred and forty years hence? or, inform us, infallibly, what will happen so distant in the future? No, the future is impenetrable to human ken. Only He who "inhabiteth eternity" knows what will surely come to pass. Therefore, we know He is the author of the Bible, for the prophecies in its pages that we know have come to pass, demonstrate the fact to us.

Let it also be noted, in this connection, how the very best formularies of so-called "Advance knowledge" relating to governmental affairs, seem to have been anticipated, prophetically, in this oldest and best of Books.

Is it not true that all the fundamental elements of constitutional law, of this and all other civilized countries, are taken from the "Mosaic Code?" Is it not true that every beneficent principle of our common law is suggested in the Decalogue?"

What approved methods of military science are taught in the schools of the foremost nations to-day, that are not to be found in the Old Testament?

Study the campaigns and extensive military operations of Moses, Joshua, and that greatest military leader the world ever saw, King David, and know that Napoleon and Wellington, and Grant and Lee, and Von Moltke, knew nothing of the science of warfare strategically that they did not know and practice.

What about the family, and civilized society? Is it not forevermore true that the best, highest and happiest state is reached when the Bible model is copied? and the Bible standard is approximated?

CHAPTER IX.

THE MIRACLE OF THE BIBLE.

> Whence but from Heaven, could men unskilled in arts,
> In several ages born, in several parts,
> Weave such agreeing truths, or how, or why,
> Should all conspire to cheat us with a lie?
> Unasked their pains, ungrateful their advice,
> Starving their gain, and martyrdom their price.
>
> DRYDEN.

The Bible is composed of sixty-six separate books; written, humanly speaking, by about thirty-eight different persons, the first and the last living quite fifteen hundred years apart. The characters of the writers, the manner and surroundings of their lives, and the situations, in every aspect of the cast of the case, make it absolutely impossible that there could have been a preconcerted plan and collusion among the agents in its construction. Yet, when the Book, as such, is examined, we find it harmonious as a whole, symmetrical in all its proportions and logically perfect. We find the same things in Revelation that we find in Genesis: The garden of God; the river of life; the tree of life; and all living creatures acting in harmony with the laws of God and at peace one with another. All in the Book that lies between, has but one bent and purpose, and that is, to bring sinful, wandering, lost man back to God and Paradise. Such a thing could not happen so, positively it could not!

Suppose that fifteen hundred years ago a man went to a marble quarry and took five blocks of marble and placed them in an open field. After he is dead many years, another man comes along and places three stones upon the five. Then two hunhundred years later another man places seven stones upon the eight; and so, through the passing years, men who never saw those who went before them in this work, bring blocks of marble from the same quarry, and place them upon the same pile, until to-day, the thirty-eighth man brings the last of sixty-six stones and places it in position on top of the other sixty-five. What would any one expect to see? Simply, and only, a pile of stones. But, suppose, instead, a statue, as perfect and artistic as ever came from the chisel of Phideas or Michael Angelo, stood before you. How could it be explained? Only in one way, viz.: That some great master artist mind planned the work, and the thirty-eight workmen simply wrought according to the known design. In just such a way was the Bible constructed. The infinitely wise God designed it, and the thirty-eight men who constructed it, were chosen by Him to execute His plans, and spake or wrote as He gave them utterance. Its construction can be explained upon no other grounds.

Again. It must be remembered that the Bible is the oldest book in the world; portions of it ante-dating, by many centuries, any other book. Also, that portions of this Book were written, humanly speaking, by ignorant and unlearned men. And yet, with all our boasted learning and progress, and the accumulated wisdom of the centuries, it stands to-day, in the estimation of the foremost Philosophers and Statesmen; Scientists and Poets; Metaphysicians and Historians; Warriors and Wise men, pre-eminently, the Book of books! The only possible reason that can be given for this very astonishing fact is that God is its Author. And yet there are those who ridicule the Book, and make light of this fact. But, is it not remarkable that among the many brilliant men who have denied the supernatural origin of the Book, not one of them has written a better one? If some one will write a better book, it will be a demonstration to the world that the Bible is, as they claim, who hate it, of human origin; and he will secure for himself such literary fame as no author ever enjoyed; and wealth by the millions. Why did not Celsus, Voltaire, Hume, or Paine write such a book? They were scholarly men, brilliant and accomplished, and industrious and prolific writers. They hated the Book with implacable hatred. They labored hard to destroy it, they had almost every possible incentive to do this. Writing a better book would have done it. Literary fame and wealth would have been theirs, had they succeeded. Why did they not do this thing? Why do not some of the bright, scholarly and gifted skeptics and haters of the Book of our day, do this thing? There is much boasting of scholarship and advanced learning by such. They tell us that this is a progressive age; that mediæval and ancient learning is as nothing compared to the learning of these days. And they are in a degree correct. Surely, then, they ought to write a better book than those nomadic men who, without libraries or universities, wrote in the very dawn of history; or, those unlettered fishermen of Galilee. And they could, and would do this very thing, were it not for the fact that God is the Author of the Bible, and it contains, therefore, infinite knowledge and wisdom.

"Where is the wise? where is the scribe? where is the disputer of this world? hath not God made foolish the wisdom of this world?" 1 Cor. 1 : 20.

Is it not true that man has improved upon everything that man ever invented or did? Place a modern "Consul" or "Mogul" locomotive engine alongside of "The Rocket," the first locomotive engine ever built, and it will be seen, at once, that great improvements have been made upon Stephenson's invention and labor.

The first sewing machine was but a crude affair. The modern sewing machine is run by electricity, and can make any article of wearing apparel worn by human beings, with almost lightning rapidity. Almost unnumbered improvements have been made upon Howe's invention.

Morse captured the idea of telegraphy, and was the first to apply it practically. But, if he were alive to-day, he would hardly know the science, it has made such rapid and great progress. The instruments now in use, in all the principal offices, would be more a cause of wonderment to him, than the first instrument he constructed was to the American people.

McCormick's invention of the reaping machine was among the greatest of modern times. But the improvements made upon it, are one hundred times more complex and remarkable than the original machine.

And it is just so with everything that man ever invented or discovered. But, the first Book still stands at the head, unimproved upon; because like all the works of God, it is not possible for man to improve upon it. Nor, can it ever be done; because like Him of Whom it treats, it is "The same yesterday, to-day and forever."

Its indestructibleness attests its supernaturalness. Men have tried in every imaginable way to destroy it. All that learning could suggest, malevolence contrive and unwearied energy accomplish, has been done to annihilate it. It looked, at one time, to those who hated the book and sought its destruction, as though their efforts would surely be rewarded with success. Voltaire said: "In one hundred years there will not be a copy of the Bible on earth." The one hundred years have passed and there are quite four hundred millions of copies of the Book, printed in more than three hundred languages and dialects, in the world to-day. There is one printed copy of the entire Book, or some portion of it, for every man, woman and child of the nearly fifteen hundred millions of the earth's population. And the very printing press on which Voltaire printed this prophecy, is owned by the Geneva Bible Society, and is used by them in printing God's Holy Word.

It seems to have thrived upon the hard treatment to which it has been subjected. I once read of an Irishman who built a stone fence for a man. When they came to a settlement for the work done, the land owner inquired: "How high did you build the fence?" "Four feet high, sir," was the response. "But are you not afraid that it will fall down?" was the second inquiry. The Irishman replied: "Well, sir, I made it five feet thick, and if it falls down, it will be higher than it was before." and just so is it with the Bible; the more it is knocked down the higher it rises.

Those who seek its destruction surely are mad! They certainly have not calculated carefully and dispassionately what would have to be done in order to accomplish this thing. In order to destroy the Bible, all printed copies and parts of the Book, and the nearly thirty thousand manuscripts would have to be destroyed. In order to do this, those who hate it would have to plunge into Arctic snows; endure Africa's heat; brave the perils of India's jungles; and, of savage tribes in the Islands of the Sea. The rice fields of China would have to be traversed; the mountains of South America climbed; and, the contagions of tropical climes faced. Into the slums of the world's great cities; where venomous serpents lurk by the way; and, where storm and shipwreck and death hold sway, wherever dying men are in darkness; there, those who love the Bible, have gone with the Sacred Volume, that despairing ones may look up and hope. But even if these journeys were made, many copies of the Bible are unpurchaseable. If they could all be bought, those who hate the Book have not money enough to buy them; or, if they had, they think too much of their money to spend it in that way. Many persons who own copies would not part from them even at the command of earth's greatest monarch. Beside, many copies could not be found though most diligent search be made.

But, suppose that all printed copies, and manuscripts were really burned, would the Bible be destroyed? By no means. In order to do this thing it would also be necessary to go into all the libraries of earth and riddle and ruin almost every book that bears the imprint of brains, for, almost every author of worth and note has incorporated into his writings some quotations from, or allusion to, the Sacred Volume. Some one has declared: "I have found four hundred and thirty-six quotations from the Bible, in the writings of Lord Alfred Tennyson." Another declared: "I have found nine hundred and twenty-six Scriptural quotations and allusions, in the writings of John Ruskin." Lord Hailes, the antiquarian, has declared: "I have actually discovered the whole New Testament except eleven verses in the secular writings of the first three centuries of this era, and I am satisfied I can find these also."

But, if this too were done, would the Bible be destroyed? By no means. In order to accomplish its destruction it would be necessary to ruin all works of the great masters in painting and mosaic; for, are not their greatest productions all, or nearly all, Scriptural incidents, truths and stories?

But would the Bible be destroyed then? By no means. Music, as well as Art, would have to be brought low. Mozart, Handel and Beethoven, and their illustrious co-laborers, would be dishonored; for, are not their majestic harmonies inseparably united with Bible truth and story?

With all this done, would the Bible be destroyed? By no means. In order to do this it would be necessary to raze to the dust of the earth every church and cathedral building; and the buildings of every educational and eleemosynary institution in the civilized world; for, these buildings are but the practical and tangible demonstration of the truth and power of the Bible.

But, if this were done, would the Bible be destroyed? By no means. In order to do this it will be necessary to go into almost every cemetery of earth and break down every monument and tombstone; for engraven upon these will be found some word, or thought, from the Bible.

And now, with all this ruin wrought, would the Bible be destroyed? By no means. In order to accomplish its utter destruction it would be necessary to annihilate every living Christian, for are they not living epistles, "known and read of all men?" I know of two men of whom it was once said by one who presumed to know, "Either of them could reproduce the Bible from memory." I have six friends any three of whom could reproduce the Bible if every copy was destroyed, I have no doubt whatever.

An Irishman, who was a Roman Catholic, somewhere and how, became possessor of a copy of the King James' version of the Bible. The Priest finding it out, called upon him and demanded of him the Book. It was handed to him and he at once threw it into the fire before which they were sitting. They both silently watched the flames consume it. When this was done "Pat" threw back his head and laughed most heartily. "Why do you laugh, you fool?" indignantly asked the Priest. Pat responded, "You think you have destroyed the Book." "Indeed I have," said the Priest. "Indeed you haven't," responded "Pat," "it is written on the fleshly tables of my heart and you can't burn it."

But, after even this was done, would the Bible be destroyed? Indeed it would not.

If this thing is ever to be done, it would be necessary to kill all unbelievers including Infidels and Atheists. I never knew an Infidel or Atheist who ever read the Bible through; but somehow, they have picked up some portion of it, and it is ineffaceably written upon the tablets of their memories.

When all these things are done—and it would be necessary to do them all in order to destroy the Bible—what would we have left? You might find a man on the coast of Labrador, with a fish-bone through his nose, who never heard about the Bible; or an almond-eyed Celestial beyond the fastnesses of the Himalayas; or a woolly-headed pilgrim, with pedals so adjusted that you must needs look at him twice in order to know which way he is traveling, in the heart of the "Dark Continent." But, as the Moravians and Bishop William Taylor are after these, and most certain to overtake them soon, unless the Destructionists desire to have things lapse into utter chaos, they must hurry the completion of their work.

Destroy the Bible! I have stood upon the north coast, lifting itself with imperial grandeur from the foundations of the earth, and watched the swellings of the sea, as with long, majestic and apparently resistless sweep, they hurled themselves, with all their prodigious energy against the pulseless bosom of the giant buttressed rocks, and, up! up!! up!!! they climbed, until their strength was well nigh gone, and then, shaking themselves into hoariness, fall backward into their own watery depths. And so, the surgings of infidel hate, with hellish and most malignant fury, have, for centuries, hurled themselves against this book—The Rock of the Eternal Ages!—only, and always, to be hurled backward into their own dark and damning depths. But the Old Rock still stands!

Julian the Apostate, Celsus, Porphyry, Voltaire, Gibbon, Hume, Bolingbroke, Chubb, Rousseau, Diderot, Paine, all men of extraordinary genius, did their utmost to destroy the Bible; but death claimed them, and they were compelled to acknowledge the claim, and they passed from their labors to give an account of themselves to God. But the Book still lives! Thrones have fallen. Dynasties have perished. Empires have disappeared in the strife of Nations. Wars and tumults; famine and pestilence; earthquake and storm; hatred and death, have characterized the passing years. But, the Book still lives!

Destroy the Bible! One might as well talk of puny man blotting the sun out of the sky! Indeed, might as well talk of annihilating God Himself, for, is it not the Eternal Logos?

Jesus said: "Heaven and earth shall pass away, but My Words shall not pass away." For

> All flesh is as grass,
> And all the glory thereof as the flower of grass.
> The grass withereth, and the flower falleth;
> But the Word of the Lord abideth forever.
> (Isa. 40: 6–8; 1 Peter 1: 24, 25.)

O, Thou blessed Word of God! Thou didst speak to me, in my ladhood, from fire-crowned, smoke-wreathed Sinai, in thunder, trumpet tones, of law, of condemnation and death. And then, when overwhelmed with a sense of my guilt and peril, I said, "Woe is me!" for I am undone and without help! In that dark hour, Thou didst speak to me, from Calvary's brow, in tones far sweeter than a mother's lullaby, of One who was judged for me,—"Suffered for sins, the just for the unjust, that he might bring us to God;" thus becoming "The end of the law unto righteousness to every one that believeth," and faith, unquestioning, said, This Word of the Gospel is true! And Life, eternal throbbed through my whole being, and hope, most glorious, has ever since been mine. I am here in an enemy's country. He has set unnumbered snares and pitfalls to entrap me and cause me to stumble. But Thou art "A lamp unto my feet and a light unto my path," that I may see how to safely make my way to the hills of God. But for Thee, I could not know the will and mind of God concerning me. Thou art "The rejoicing of my heart;" for "I rejoice," in Thee, "As one that findeth great spoil." Thou art more to me "Than my necessary food." Thou art "Sweeter" to me "Than honey, and than the drippings of the honey comb." "O how love I" Thee! "I will ever make Thee the Man of my counsel," and the strength of my years. My father loved Thee, and from his boyhood followed in Thy precepts to do them; and, when dying he clasped Thee to his heart; and, when we laid him away, to rest until Jesus comes, we placed Thee under his head for a pillow. My dear mother has loved Thee for quite seventy years, and hoped in Thy truth; and, now, after nearly four score years of journeying, she sits where the shadows are lengthening into twilight, rejoicing the while the light from the throne of God falls upon her sweet though furrowed face. The best and truest of all ages have loved Thee. I love

Thee! If there were one drop of blood in my veins that did not throb in intensest loyality to Thee, I would let it out if it were the last. Go on Thy way, Thou message from the skies; dissipate earth's darkness and gloom; banish ignorance and superstition, and everywhere, among all peoples, let Thy cleansing, saving power be felt, until the whole world shall be filled with "The light of the knowledge of the glory of God in the face of Jesus Christ."

CHAPTER X.

SUPPLEMENTAL DISCUSSION—THE PENTATEUCH.

The Higher Critics are nearly of one mind as to the "Compilation Theory,"—that is, they nearly all accept it. But, this family of Hupfelds, though so young, has grown almost beyond recognition, and continues to increase. The case as it now stands, is about as follows: They hold that those portions of the first five books of the Bible where the name of God (Elohim) is used, were written by an Elohistic writer, whom they designate as E. That the passages where the name Lord (Jehovah) is used, were written by a Jehovistic writer, whom they designate as J. The absurdity of such a division of these sacred writings was made evident, when attention was called to the fact that these names were used again and again, not only in the same paragraph, but in the same sentence, as for instance: Gen. 7: 16, "And they that went in, went in male and female of all flesh, as Elohim commanded him : and Jehovah shut him in." Gen. 24: 3, "And I will make thee swear by Jehovah, the Elohim of heaven." And, Gen. 28: 21. "Then shall Jehovah be my Elohim." Common sense demanded, at this point, that the Critics should abandon their theory; but, no, they simply said: "Such passages prove that there was a third writer, combining the styles of the 'Elohistic' and 'Jehovistic' writers, and we will call Him J. E."

Then these gentlemen thought they discovered that the first chapter of Genesis, about half of Exodus and five-sixths of Leviticus were written about eight hundred years after Moses; and, because they treated largely of priestly legislation, therefore, they must have been written by one person; and inasmuch as the names Elohim and Jehovah occur many, many times in these portions of the Word, they call these writings the "Priest's Code," and the writer the Priestly Elhoist, or the P. E.

Then they say a "Deutronomist" writer wrote all the later legislative portions of the books, and they call him D.

After the Children of Israel returned from the Babylonish Captivity, a "Redactor," whom they call R., redacted all these writings into their present shape; and that, which to an ordinary mind constitutes a sublime unity, the Pentateuch, was thus edited.

It is true that a very few of these gentlemen believe that Moses did write a small portion of these five books. Some say ten chapters; some more, some less; but, the vast majority insist that Moses had nothing whatever to do with these writings. One of the arguments against the Mosaic authorship is this: that writing was not known in the days of Moses. Unfortunately for this, in explorations made recently in Egypt, extensive correspondence was discovered, evidently written one hundred and fifty years before the time of Moses. Thus does the Almighty Himself come to the rescue of His own Word; and causes the very stones to speak in refutation of theories advanced by our rationalistic critics.

These gentlemen don't pretend to tell us who are E., and J., and J. E., and P. E. and D., and R. They have no proof that such persons ever existed. They are only imaginary personages. The Critics simply insist that Moses did not write these books; and, as it is pretty certain that somebody did, they invented writers to suit their views of the case. They are pure fabrications.

Joshua, Caleb, Gideon, Samuel, David, Solomon, The Prophets, Jesus, Peter, John, James, Jude and Paul, knew nothing whatever of E., J., J E., P. E., D., and R. The Church Fathers and Reformers were in like ignorance of their existence. And fifty years hence they will not be known, or thought of, save as among the curious vagaries of human conceits.

Let us now turn from the opinions and conjectures of men, to the explicit testimony of the Highest Critics.

THE TESTIMONY OF JESUS.

In Matt. viii, 4, He said: "Moses commanded" the things in Lev. xiv, 1–12. In Matt. xix, 7, 8, He said: "Moses commanded" and "Moses * * * suffered you" the things mentioned in Deut. xxiv, 1. In Mark vii, 10, He said: Moses said, Honor thy father and thy mother," quoting from Exod. xx, 10. In Mark xii, 26, He said: "Have ye not read in the book of Moses?" and then quotes Exod. iii, 6.

In John vii, 19, 22, 23, He said: "Did not Moses give you the law? * * * Moses therefore gave unto you circumcision, * * * the law of Moses." This law is recorded in Lev. xii, 3.

Of course those who accept the words of Jesus as true will not doubt that Moses wrote the Pentateuch; but those who disbelieve it will not accept the testimony of Jesus, for He said: "For had ye believed Moses, ye would have believed Me; for he wrote of Me. But if ye believe not his writings, how shall ye believe My words?" (John v, 46, 47.)

Dr. Leacock has put the case in the following manner, and it is none too emphatic or strong:

"Accepting the judgment of the Critics, we have before us two alternatives regarding Jesus: He was either ignorant of the facts, and hence taught error under a misapprehension; or else He knew the facts, and knowingly taught what was false, and thus helped to fasten a fraud and a lie upon His nation and His after Church.

"It is impossible to accept the first of these suppositions. He to whom the Spirit was given without measure—He who needed not that any should testify of man, for He knew what was in man—He who, before Abraham was born, had existence—He who was with the Father from the beginning, and was before all things, He surely could not be ignorant of the true history of these books. If therefore we accept Jesus as the only begotten Son, and one with the Father, we must dismiss this first supposition concerning Him.

"We turn then to the other proposition, viz., that knowing the facts He suppressed them, and taught what He knew to be false, and linked Himself with those who had conspired to fasten upon the Jewish nation and upon the world, a fraud and a lie. Can this be so? Is Jesus a fraud? Is he a liar? Then good-bye to His religion. If he is false in one particular, why not in all? We have no security. The foundations are swept away, for everything centers in Him and depends upon His truthfulness. If He is not "*the truth*," then our hope is gone. Let us eat and drink, for to-morrow we die.

"This is disaster overwhelming that these learned critics are trying to bring upon us. They remind us of poor blind Samson putting forth his strength to drag down the columns that supported the roof over his head. There is this difference—they know not what they do. Nor have they Samson's strength. We may dismiss our fears, and still look to Jesus with unshaken confidence. "Heaven and earth shall pass away; but My words shall not pass away."

THE TESTIMONY OF THE HOLY SPIRIT.

The internal evidence, in part, is as follows: In Exodus 17: 14, He said: "And the Lord said unto Moses, Write this for a memorial in a [the] Book, and rehearse it in the ears of Joshua." In Exodus 34: 27–28, He said: "And the Lord said unto Moses, Write thou these words: for after the tenor of these words have I made a covenant with thee and with Israel; * * * and he wrote upon the tables the words of the covenant, the ten commandments" (words). In Num. 33: 2, He said: "And Moses wrote their goings out according to their journeys." In Deut. 31: 9, 22–24, He said: "And Moses wrote this law. * * *. Moses therefore wrote this song the same day. * * * When Moses had made an end of writing the words of this law in a [the] Book."

The things said to have been written by Moses, in the above passages, relate to the giving of the law, the wars, various festivals, etc., belonging to the history of Israel during the desert wanderings.

In Josh. 11: 12, he said: "As Moses commanded" (See Deut. 7: 1–2). In Judges 1: 20, he said: "As Moses had spoken" (see Deut. 1: 36). In 1 Kings 8: 53, he said: "Thou spakest by the hand of Moses." Reference is here made to Deut. 12: 10–11. In 1 Chron. 6: 49, the things mentioned are in Lev. 1: 1–9, and it is declared that " Moses * * * commanded it." In 2 Chron. 33: 8, we have the statement: "The statutes and ordinances by the hand of Moses;" in chap. 34: 14, "The book of the law of the Lord given by Moses;" and in chap. 35: 6: "According to the word of the Lord by the hand of Moses." Reference in these three passages is made to Exod. 12. In Ezra 3: 2, we have the statement that Deut. 12, 5–6, was given by Moses. In Neh. 8: 14, we are informed that Lev. 23, 34–43, and Deut. 16: 13, were by the " hand of Moses;" and in chap. 9: 14, it is stated that Exod. 20:8, was also "by the hand of Moses." Dan. 9, 11–13, tells us that Deut. 28: 15–68, and Lev. 26: 14–39, are "in the law of Moses."

Acts 3:22, says: "Moses indeed said," and the quotation is from Deut. 18:15. In Rom. 10:5, (Rev. Ver.), we have: "For Moses writeth" (see Lev. 18:5); and in chap. 10:19, it is declared: "Moses said" (Deut. 32:21.) In 1 Cor. 9:9, he said: "It is written in the law of Moses," and then quotes Deut. 25:4. In 2 Cor. 3:15, he said: "Whensoever Moses is read." The things of which he here speaks are found in Exod. 34:29–35. In Heb. 9:19, reference is made to Exod. 24:4–8, where it is said: "And Moses wrote all the words of the Lord." In Rev. 15:3 he says that Deut. 32: 1–43, or Exod. 15:1–18, is "the song of Moses."

In the above citations I have not exhausted the testimony of the Highest Critics on this subject by any means; nor have I given the testimony of the Sadducees, who declared that Moses wrote Deut. 25:5 (see Matt. 22:24); nor of the Pharisees, who said Lev. 12:2 was given by Moses (see Luke 2:22); nor of John the Baptist, who said: "The law was given by Moses" (John 1:17); nor yet of Philip, who said: "We have found Him of whom Moses * * * did write" (John 1:45), all of whom were certainly as well qualified to testify on this subject as the Higher Critics.

Of course, the testimony of the Holy Spirit will not count with most of these gentlemen, because they practically deny His office work in these words.

The fact is, they are compelled to deny the supernatural in the Bible. They dare not say the Bible is uninspired; and so they have certain theories which at the bottom, eliminate all supernatural elements, and practically deny real inspiration. Hence the vigor of their assaults upon verbal inspiration. Their working postulates degrade the Bible to the level of human productions. They will, therefore, brush aside these testimonies of the Holy Spirit, by insisting that, if He had anything to do with the matter, He was so completely dominated by the human characteristics of the writers, that the accuracy and truthfulness of the record, cannot be relied upon. This is, logically, the inevitable result of their theories of inspiration.

As between the testimony of the Highest and "Higher Critics," no one who is loyal to God's Holy Word, will hesitate for a single moment to choose. No one appreciates more than I the great labor of those scholarly men who have devoted their great learning, with indomitable wills, to ascertain the exact text of the Scriptures; but, when they set up their judgment against the plain and explicit statements of the Highest Critics, then is "scholarship run mad," and all Christians should part company with them.

Not a few ministers study the "Higher Critics" more than the Highest. There is a notion among some of them that, unless they agree with the conclusions of these learned men, they will not themselves be considered scholarly. Just here is a very great peril. The minister, of all men, ought to be careful to "prove all things," and "hold fast that which is good," remembering that "If we receive the witness of men, the witness of God is greater."

Human leadership in such matters is unsafe. We can know the truth without the "Higher Critics." Jesus said: "Howbeit when He the Spirit of truth is come He will guide you into all truth" (John 16: 13.) And the testimony of the Holy Spirit is this: "But the anointing which ye have received of Him abideth in you, and ye need not that any man teach you: but as the same anointing teacheth you of all things and is truth, and is no lie, and even as it hath taught you, ye shall abide in Him" (1 John 2: 27.)

The numerous and persistent attacks made upon the integrity of the Pentateuch are not surprising when we remember the defeat Satan suffered in contending with Michael the archangel for possession of the body of Moses, and the repulse Jesus gave him in the wilderness struggle, with the "Sword of the Spirit," by quoting three times from Deuteronomy.

The Higher Criticism is having full swing just now. There is much of "a fad" in it. It will soon be a curiosity among wornout speculations.

Long after the present school of "Higher Critics" shall be forever forgotten, the testimony of the Highest Critics as to the editorship of the Pentateuchal books will be believed by the good and true of all nations. "The word of the Lord abideth forever." Let us possess our souls in patience.

CHAPTER XI.

JOB.

Concerning the book of Job the Higher Critics teach that it is a fictitious drama, representing an Oriental debate between dark eyed Sheiks in their tent, on the ways of Providence or the mysteries of God's moral administration. They say it is only fictitious like the parables of the Old Testament, and that of the Rich Man and Lazarus in the New. The view to-day is, that it was a part of the Chochma or Wisdom Literature, and written either in the time of Solomon, or in post-exile times.

Some of the Critics, however, quote the different views of the Talmud as to the authorship of the Book. Some saying it was composed in the time of Moses and by him; others in time of Abraham; others in time of Jacob; others in time of Esther; and still others in time of David. All these, save that it was written in time of Moses, and by Moses, are the merest conceits. It is exceeding curious to notice how these critics despise all reference to the Talmud as worthless when it does not support their views, but cling to it as deserving of consideration when it does. The fatal postulate with the Higher Critics now, is that it makes no difference who wrote the Biblical Books! They teach that the authority of any part of the Bible does not depend upon the knowledge of the "Authorship," but only on the fact that it is in the Canon. Its claim to a place in the Canon does not rest upon its authorship. This is destructive to the last degree, of the value of the tradition of the church, and of the authority of the Apostles. Such a rule would admit the Apocrypha into the Canon. If the Jewish Church ever received a Book into the Canon, it was *because its author was known* as an inspired writer. We of to-day may not have the evidence who that author was; but the Church that received the Book as a part of God's Word had it. The early tradition of the Church is therefore of great value, and not to be set aside by speculative criticism of men who hold lightly the doctrine of Inspiration.

There are, apparently, a few valid reasons for believing that Moses was the writer of the Book; but, the preponderance of evidence is against such view and clearly in favor of a pre-Mosaic authorship.

There is not sufficient proof either from the literary style, or contents, or form, that it was a production written after the entrance into Canaan. It belongs on its very face to the times of the Patriarchs, and the philosophical discussions of the "Sons of the East." It was not possible for a Jew, living in Solomonian or post-exile times, in Palestine, to produce a work like this. No post-Solomonian writer could reproduce the times before Moses as here; nor keep himself so completely as not to betray by something the Hebrew times in which he lived. The whole physiognomy of the

Book is Arabian, is of the East, and the desert, in its minutest features, without one solitary kind of Jewish life, custom or mode of thought. The entire manner of discussion is as different from the Jewish manner of debate, as it is from the manner of discussion among the Greeks and the Romans.

The following are some of many specific *reasons* for believing that the Book is pre-Mosaic:

First—The length of life peculiar to the time.

Second—The worship of Sun, Moon and Stars and no mention of idols.

Third—Riches reckoned by cattle.

Fourth—The head of the family is priest.

Fifth—The kind of coin mentioned.

Sixth—The musical instruments mentioned.

Seventh—No sacrifices such as are named in the Pentateuch mentioned.

Eighth—No reference, whatever, to the Mosaic law.

Ninth—No reference to the Exodus. When it is remembered that no fact in ancient Jewish history is so frequently and prominently referred to in nearly all the Old Testament books, as this, the entire absence of any statement concerning this most important fact in the history of God's chosen people, or allusion to it in Job, is an unanswerable argument in favor of the un-Jewish and pre-Mosaic origin of the Book.

Tenth—No allusion to a Jew, or a Hebrew, or the Holy land, or Jerusalem, or the Tabernacle, or the Temple. All this adds emphasis to the ninth argument, and is strikingly significant.

Eleventh—The expression "Sons of God."
Twelfth—The philosophy of Temah.
Thirteenth—The manner of discussion.
Fourteenth—It is highly probable that some of the parties who are prominently named in Job were identified with the times immediately following Abraham, Isaac and Jacob. In Gen. 36: 4, 10, mention is made of Eliphaz, as a son of Esau. And Esau and his descendants lived in Mount Seir and beyond in the way of the east. "Bildad the Shuhite,' whose appellation, "the Shuhite," may connect him with Shuah, the sixth son of Abraham by Keturah (Gen. 25: 2). The sons of Abraham by Keturah occupied the country towards the Persian Gulf. Also "Elihu the Buzite." If he descended from "Buz," a son of Nahor, as seems quite probable—See Gen. 22: 21—he was a nephew of Abraham. The family of "Buz" also settled in the borders of the Arabian desert. See Jer. 25: 23. In Gen. 10: 29, and 1 Chron. 1: 23, mention is made of Jobab, the son of Zerah, the son of Esau. In Smith's Bible Dictionary we are told: "That in a notice appended to the Alexandrian version it is stated: "He (Job) bore previously the name of Jobab;" and that a tradition adopted by the Jews and some Christian Fathers, identified Job with Jobab, prince of Edom, mentioned in Gen. 36: 33. The names of Abram, Jacob and Joshua were changed; and, taking the above-mentioned things into the account it is very probable that Job was once called Jobab. This places him in the time of

Eliphaz, Bildad and Elihu, all of whom were, without doubt, descendants of Abraham and sons of the east. The Book itself is identified with these personages and times. Ewald asserts very positively that in all the descriptions of manners and customs, domestic, social and political, and even in the indirect allusions and illustrations, the genuine coloring of the age of Job is of the period between Abraham and Moses; and that all historical examples and allusions are taken exclusively from patriarchal times. M. Renan, Hahn, Schlottman, and other critics fully agree with this opinion.

Fifteenth—In Job 30: 1-7, the Bushmen are mentioned. They belonged to a very early age, and doubtless disappeared before the time of Moses. The plain inference from the above passage is, that the writer must have known them from his own personal observation.

The position of the Critics that this Book is a parable, is, like most of their working rules, but an audacious assumption. The personality of Job is clearly and most positively established by the Lord God. In Ezekiel 14: 14 it is said: "Though these three men, Noah, Daniel and Job were in it (the land of Israel), they should deliver but their own souls by their righteousness, saith the Lord God." Mark, it is "The Lord God" who here speaks; and what He says utterly refutes the assumption of the Critics that Job is a "Fictitious character."

Besides this, the Holy Spirit, by the Apostle James, speaks thus upon this matter: "Ye have heard of the patience of Job, and have seen the end of the Lord, that the Lord is very pitiful, and of tender mercy." Jas. v: 11. Can any one with unbiased and unprejudiced mind read the above quotation and doubt the personality of Job? Is it possible that the Holy Spirit had any other than a historical person in mind when He indited these words?

Parables were used by our Lord as illustrations. In their structure and distinctive characteristics they are uniformly and as truly unlike the Book of Job as the Sermon on the Mount. Therefore the declaration that the Book is a parable is a bare and bold assumption.

The Book of Job belongs to a time far too early for works of fiction. The earliest writings are chronological and historical. It is demonstrably true that fiction belongs to a much later age—to a time when authorship, by well known laws of development, became an art. In order to meet this argument, the Critics are compelled to assign the work to post-exile times.

The singular air of reality in the entire record makes it quite improbable that any one with an unbiased mind could believe it to be fictitious. If it is fictitious a Jew must have written it. Uz was in no way associated with Israelitish history. These peoples were unfriendly, if not, indeed enemies. Is it thinkable that a Jew would have made such heroes as this Book contains of an unfriendly race?

The uniqueness, beauty and incomparable merits

of the work all must admit. Carlyle says: "Apart from all theories about it, I call the Book of Job one of the grandest things ever written with a pen." Froude speaks of Job as a "Book of which it is to say little to call it unequaled of its kind, and which will one day, perhaps, when it is allowed to stand on its own merits, be seen towering up alone, far away above all the poetry of the world." The Critics ignore the Supernatural in their working rules. The Sacred Writings are subjected to the same tests as the writings of men, and thus degraded to the same level. But these gentlemen don't try to explain why this oldest writing stands to-day unequaled as a literary production and commands such testimonies as the above. Judged by any established law of criticism, of the progress and development of literature, and only one conclusion can be reached, viz.: it has a Supernatural origin—God is its Author.

CHAPTER XII.

THE PSALMS.

It is a first principle with the "Higher Critics" to set aside even the most venerated and well established tradition and belief of the Jewish Church as to the authorship and purport of the Psalms, and decide for themselves, their date, origin, occasion, authorship and meaning on purely internal grounds, and their own evolutionary construction of the history of Israel. The so called "Scientific Criticism" that assigned the Pentateuch to unknown authors and redactors from eight hundred to one thousand years after Moses was dead, finds no difficulty in doing a like service for the Psalms of King David. The deniers of Supernatural Inspiration, who limit the prophetic gift, or foreknowledge of the Prophet to his own "Historical situation," find it easy not only to put David's Harp in the hands of some romantic Maccabean, but to protest that David never wrote the Psalms which are expressly ascribed to him, in the titles, although our Lord and His Apostles say he did! For instance, since their imaginary *"Elohistic writer,"* as they call him, *i. e.*, the author of Psalms where the name God is used, did not live *until after the exile*, it is a necessity with them to put their "God-Psalms" as they call them down, at as low a date as possible, even into Maccabean times, *i. e.*, 170–160 B.C. When evangelical men object to these critics that in many of the Davidic Psalms and which are expressly ascribed to David, there are clear references to the Pentateuch and a constant use of the name "Elohim," they meet the objection by simply saying that David never wrote these Psalms, and that Christ and His Apostles were mistaken in thinking that he did! They take advantage of the fact that quite a number of the Psalms are anonymous. They do more; they are so bold as to contradict the titles of Psalms that are not anonymous. They say that all the titles of the Psalms are pure inventions of late redactors or compilers. They say the Hebrew Psalter gives to David fewer Psalms than the Septuagent Version without explaining why. They cite the fancies of some Talmudist and a few evangelical commentators, as to certain Psalms, and represent as their critical conviction what was merely a transient speculation. They review the judgment of the official custodians of the Sacred Oracles, the judgment of centuries, and assert that, because successive editions of the Psalms were made as the Psalmody increased, therefore the men of Solomon's time, and Hezekiah's time, and Ezra's and Nehemiah's time, were ignorant of just what Psalms David wrote. These collectors made blunders, it is said, in their selections, as they did in their titles, and transmitted to us a Psalter the arrangement and contents of which not only deceived the Jewish people, the Sanhedrim, the Scribes, the Elders and the Priests, but Christ, the Apostles and the whole Christian Church, and will not stand the tests of literary and historical criticism for one hour! Some of them go so far as to say that Christ and His Apostles were the dupes of the later synagogue, and of Scribes who tampered with the Hebrew Bible; and that they accommodated themselves to the "tendency of the times which was to ascribe everything to Moses or David."

The audacity of some of these gentlemen is indeed startling. That which is sacred to the thought and heart of millions of the most holy and intelligent people the world over, and, which has been venerated for ages, is disposed of with as little ceremony as though it were a fable, or, they, themselves, were the disciples of Voltaire. Their arbitrary disposition of the traditions of the church is alarming; and, their arrogant assumption that scholarship is all with them, is the most stupendous specimen of "cheek," of modern times.

Let us now look into the case and then examine the testimony of the Highest Critics. The threefold division of the Old Testament was "Moses, the Prophets and the Writings." "Moses" meant the Pentateuch. The "Prophets" meant not only the prophetical but also the historical books of the Old Testament, for the Prophets were the Historiographers of Israel. The "Psalms" stood at the head of the third great division which included all the rest of the Jewish Scriptures, and gave to the whole collection their name. Besides this they were called simply the "Writings" (Kethubim) or "Hagiographa," the "Sacred Writings." The fact that the Psalms were classed with the "Kethubim," or third great division—as was also the prophecy of Daniel—did not mean that this division was inferior in authority to the preceding, for "every Scripture is God-breathed," and was so regarded by the Jews. From Moses to Malachi all was of divine authority. The inspiration of the Word of God is not the illumination of mere natural genius such as we see in Homer, Dante, or Milton, but was a supernatural enduement by the Holy Spirit. It was this inspiration that gave us the Psalms.

The arrangement of the Psalms is very remarkable. Prof. Delitzsch says: "The Psalter is a Pentateuch, the echo of the Five Books of Moses, from the heart of Israel. It is the five Books of the Church to Jehovah as the law is the Five Books of Jehovah to the Church." This is a wonderful correspondence, and was noticed by the Fathers of the Church. Hyppolytus was clear that "This five-fold division of the Psalms was made with reference to the Pentateuch." The division is as follows:

Book I. This contains 41 Psalms, *i. e.*, 1-41. Of these, 37 are expressly ascribed to David as their author. Psalms 10 and 33 which are anonymous are nevertheless Davidic, as they are simply the continuation of Psalms 9 and 32. The two introductory Psalms, 1 and 2, though anonymous, are clearly Davidic, for Peter quotes the Second Psalm as a Psalm of David, Acts 4 : 25-27, and, by all interpreters, Psalms 1 and 2 are regarded as but parts of but one Psalm. Thus the whole 41 are genuine Psalms of David. The prevailing name of God is "Jehovah." It is a harmless thing to call them "Jehovistic Psalms," but the conclusion drawn by the "Higher Critics" that the author of Psalms that have the name of Elohim as the prevailing name was not David, is but a bold assumption and not to be tolerated one moment.

Book II. This contains 30 Psalms, *i. e.*, from 42 to 72, inclusive. It begins with 7 Psalms for the Sons of Korah. Psalm 43 is part of Psalm 42. Both are anonymous. There is no solid argument against their Davidic authorship. Psalm 50 is a Psalm of Asaph. Then come 21 Psalms of David, *i. e.*, from 51 to 72. Psalms 66, 67 and 71 are anonymous, but are nevertheless Davidic. Psalm 72, concerning, or with reference to Solomon, is undoubtedly a Psalm of David. So that, save the Asaph Psalm, this whole group belongs to David. The prevailing name of God, is Elohim. Hence they are called "Elohistic Psalms."

Book III. This contains 16 psalms, *i.e.*, from 73 to 89, inclusive. It begins with eleven Psalms of Asaph, *i. e.*, from 73 to 84. Then come four Psalms for the Sons of Korah, all Davidic, *i. e.*, from 85 to 88. Psalm 89 belongs to Ethan. Sometimes the name "Jehovah," and sometimes the name Elohim, is used.

Book IV. This, also, contains 16 Psalms, *i. e.*, from 90 to 106, inclusive. It begins with the oldest Psalm, the only Psalm anterior to David in the whole collection. Its author was "Moses, the man of God." Its historical occasion was the end of the wilderness-wandering and the sentence of death recorded in Numbers 14: 28, etc. The rest of this group are anonymous, except Psalm 101 and 103, which are expressly ascribed to David. "Jehovah" is the only name used here.

Book V. This contains 43 Psalms, *i. e.*, from 107 to 150 inclusive. Of these, 15 are expressly assigned to David, viz.: 108, 109, 110; 122, 124, 131, 133; 138-145. Psalm 127 is assigned to Solomon. Psalms 111-113, 115-117, and 146-150, eleven in all, are Hallelujah Psalms, *i. e.*, beginning or ending with "Praise ye the Lord!" The great Mercy Psalm is Psalm 136, in which the Lord's mercy is celebrated twenty-six times. The anonymous Psalms are 107, 111-114; 118-121, 123, 125-130, 132, 134, 136, 137, 146-150; twenty-five in all. Several of these are clearly Davidic because continuing the preceding one which is ascribed to David. Others are demonstrably so, from their style and contents, even without a title. The Jews call the anonymous Psalms "Orphan Psalms." The prevailing name in this group is "Jehovah." In this group there are fifteen "Pilgrim Psalms," or "Songs of Degrees," viz.: from 120 to 134.

Such are the divisions of the five-fold Psalter. Of these, 75 Psalms are expressly assigned to David and a large majority of the rest are clearly his, even without a title; one to Moses, one to Solomon, 12 to Asaph, eleven for the "Sons of Korah," one to Heman, one to Ethan, 15 Pilgrim Songs, eleven Hallelujah Psalms, or 12 if we include the great

"Mercy Psalm;" 51 are anonymous; 34 have no title or superscription — the "Orphan Psalms." These "Orphan Psalms" the Talmud, Hilary, Jerome and others, assign to the author named immediately preceding. The fancy of the Septuagint Version that they are to be distributed to Jeremiah, Ezekiel, Haggai and Zechariah has no historical foundation. Far more likely they are parts of systems of Psalms whose authors names are given.

When it is said that David wrote the Psalms, and the New Testament cites the Psalms as the "Words of David," this does not mean that David wrote all the Psalms, for some are expressly assigned to other authors—to Moses, Solomon, Asaph, Heman and Ethan. Some have superscriptions or titles, others are anonymous. The designation of the whole collection took its name from David, the chief author, just as the name Ephraim was given to the ten tribes because Ephraim was the greatest of them all. The most of the anonymous Psalms are indisputably the Psalms of David, as even an ordinary English reader might tell, from their tone, spirit, style and historical occasions. Every Psalm quoted by our Lord and His Apostles, as by David, was really such. Some, even without a title to them, are ascribed to David in the New Testament. The second Psalm is an instance of this, and this determines the authorship of the first Psalm, for the original unity of both, as one Psalm, is admitted. Whatever disputes the Critics may raise as to the value of the superscriptions, the words of Christ and His Apostles are authority that should be unhesitatingly recognized by all professing Christians. The rejection of the authorship of certain Davidic Psalms by certain critics, the denial of the authenticity of others on purely speculative grounds, or on a false view of Jewish history; the assertion that the titles and doxologies are inventions of compilers and redactors; the attempt to invalidate Davidic authorship by setting up a non-correspondence of the Psalms with the personality and times of David, and the relegation of Psalms to a date low down as the Maccabees, ought to be resisted in the interest of true criticism as directly in the face of all tradition and of the authority of Christ Himself.

It is an unscholarly criticism, as even a half-scholar might easily see to conclude that, because certain Psalms are anonymous therefore they were not written by King David. There is an order and an authorship, often not hard to be recognized, even where everything at first sight seems to be arbitrary and fortuitous. As Prof. Binney of Aberdeen says: "In not a few of the anonymous Psalms the hand of David may be distinctly traced." Dr. J. A. Alexander says: "The authorship is not always as obscure as at first sight it might seem. There are pairs of Psalms where the author's name is found only with the first. We may trace not only pairs but *trilogies*. And even more extensive *systems of Psalms*, each independent of the rest, particularly when the nucleus or the basis of the series is an ancient Psalm—for instance, one of David's to which others are added." Hengstenberg tells us that "David was the author of the alphabetic Psalms, and to him belongs the formation of the *pairs* of Psalms, and the larger *Psalm-cycles.*" Prof. Sayce tells us that the men of Hezekiah's time collected all the Psalms of David and those of other Psalmists "from the Temple-Library." See 2 Chron. 29:30; and Neh. 12:46. Is it at all likely that the best educated men of Israel, editing the Psalms of David and of Asaph, under the very eyes of Isaiah, the greatest of all the prophets—a preacher in the Temple—did not know what the Psalms of David were? The words of Dr. J. A. Alexander, believed by many competent judges to be the ablest scholar of this generation, ought to have weight with seekers after truth. He says: "All the attempts so strenuously made by modern Critics to discredit the inscriptions to the Psalms as spurious additions of a later date, containing groundless conjectures often at variance with the terms and substance of the Psalm itself, are defeated by the fact that they are found in the Hebrew text, as far back as we can trace it, not as addenda, but as integral parts of the composition." And, again: "The Psalms were not thrown together at random, but adjusted by a careful hand. The modern critics have tasked their ingenuity to prove that the Psalms are separate and detached collections, contemporaneous or successive, by unknown authors and combined afterwards to form the present Psalter. But they have never been able to account for the remarkable position of the "Psalms of David" in all parts of the book, a book whose five-fold arrangement dates from Ezra, whom uniform tradition and analogy agree in representing as the inspired collector of the Canon—a competent, rather, an infallible authority."

Let us now examine the testimony of the Highest Critics. The last question our Lord put to the Pharisees was this: "What think ye of Christ? Whose Son is He?" They answered, "David's Son." Very well, said Jesus, "If David in Spirit, *i. e.*, if King David by inspiration of the Holy Spirit calls Him 'Lord,' how is He David's Son?" The one hundred and tenth Psalm says: "Jehovah said unto Adonai, sit on my right hand until I make thine enemies thy footstool." If Messiah is David's Son, how is He David's Lord? There was only one answer to this, and the Pharisees, who certainly understood Hebrew, saw it and refused to make it. It was that Messiah should be both God and man in one person. They felt the force of it. They were silenced, for the whole nation admitted that the Psalm was Messianic, and that David was its author, and spoke by the Holy Spirit. The Lord vindicated His claim to Deity and Messiahship by appeal to the inspired words of the King of Israel. Let it be noticed that Christ refers to this in Matt. 22:41-46; Mark 12:35-37, and Luke 20:41-44. Peter referred to it on the Day of Pentecost. See Acts 2:34-36. Paul also mentions it in Heb. 1:3, 4, 13. All say the Psalm is a prophecy concerning Jesus

Christ, and given by David through whom the Holy Spirit spoke. We learn from these passages (1) that "David Himself" spoke the Psalm; (2) that the "Holy Spirit" by the "Mouth of David" said it, "David in the Spirit," "David in the Holy Spirit," (3) that the Psalm was what "God" said; (4) and that David, Jesus Christ, Peter, Paul and the Holy Spirit are a unit in this testimony.

Now, what says the "Higher Criticism?" It flatly denies all this, and teaches that David never wrote the Psalm; that the Holy Spirit had nothing to do with it; that the Jewish nation was deluded in thinking it to be Messianic; that Jesus did not know any better, not being a Higher Critic; that both Peter and Paul, as well as Christ, were simply the victims of an old and popular idea; and that we, imitating them, are no better than they. Here it is in their own words: "It is usual to take this Psalm as Messianic, and interpret it of Messiah's warfare and exaltation. The New Testament is cited as proof of this. Our Lord Himself says that David wrote it with regard to a greater than himself; that is, the expected Messiah. Again, it is alleged that Peter in the Acts, takes the Messianic import for granted. But Christ did not meddle with critical questions connected with the Old Testament, as His mission was of another character. He simply acquiesced in the current views of such questions, as long as they did not affect the nature of that mission * * * In regard to the Apostles, we cannot in all cases, adopt their interpretations of the Old Testament, since they were not infallible. The Psalm probably refers to the Maccabean times, and to one of the Hasmonean Princes, such as Jonathan." (HEBRAICA, April, 1889, p. 102.)

What are we here told? That Jesus Christ was an ignorant man in matters of authorship and exegesis. That two days before His death He applied to Himself, in proof of His Deity and Messiahship, and in view of His resurrection and ascension to God's right hand, a military poem that referred to a brother of Judas Maccabeus, that was not written by David at all, but by some one unknown to the world, nearly nine hundred years after King David's death; and, that the testimony of the Holy Spirit by the Apostles is false, and, therefore, not to be believed. In my humble judgment this is destructive to the last degree, and comes perilously near blasphemy against the Holy Ghost.

In Acts 1: 15, 16 we are informed that Peter said that "David spake" the things recorded in Psalm 41:9. On the Day of Pentecost he said: "For David saith concerning Him, 'I beheld the Lord always before my face; for He is on my right hand that I should not be moved; therefore my heart was glad and my tongue rejoiced; moreover my flesh also shall dwell in hope, because Thou wilt not leave my soul in Hades; neither wilt Thou suffer Thy Holy One to see corruption. * * * Being therefore a prophet * * * he foreseeing this spake,'" etc., etc. Acts 2: 25–32. Notice the explicit statements of Peter: "David saith;" "therefore being a prophet;" "he (David) foreseeing this spake." According to this testimony David wrote the Sixteenth Psalm. If he did not, Peter lied. I believe he told the truth, for he had a mouth and wisdom, which all his adversaries were not able to withstand or to gainsay.

When Peter and John returned to their own company after imprisonment and dire threatening, the disciples with one accord said: "Who by the Holy Ghost, by the mouth of our father David thy servant, didst say," and then they quote Psalm 2: 1, 2 (see Acts 4: 25, 26). If David did not write the first and second verses of the second Psalm, "By the Holy Ghost," the Apostles bore false testimony. I believe they knew what they were talking about, and that they told the truth.

Paul, writing by the Holy Spirit, says: "Even as David also pronounceth blessing upon the man, unto whom God reckoneth righteousness apart from works, saying: 'Blessed are they whose iniquities are forgiven, and whose sins are covered. Blessed is the man to whom the Lord will not reckon sin.'" Rom. 4:6–8. The quotation is from Psalm 32: 1, 2; and Paul says that David is the author of what is there said. I believe Paul told the truth.

In Rom. 11: 9, 10, Paul says explicitly that David said the things uttered in Psalm 69: 22, 23.

In Heb. 4: 7, we are informed that David is the author of Psalm 95: 7, 8.

We here have the unequivocal testimony of the Highest Critics that King David was the author of parts—and if of parts, certainly of the whole—of the second, sixteenth, thirty-second, forty-first, ninety-fifth and one hundred and tenth Psalms. To deny this is to impeach the testimony of the Son of God, the Holy Ghost, and of the Apostles.

Many of these critics not only deny the Davidic authorship of the Psalms, but that they contain any Messianic prophecy whatever. Here are a few specimens: " Psalm 88. This Psalm is not Messianic. A suffering Messiah is unknown to the Old Testament." " Psalm 109. This Psalm is not Messianic; neither can the use of it by Peter, as recorded in the Acts, make it apply to Jesus! And it does not suit the character of David, as if he were the author speaking prophetically." " Psalm 118. This Psalm was applied to Messiah at the time of Christ, as the citation of the twenty-second verse, in the Gospels and the Acts show. But it is not necessary to suppose, on that account, that such was the original sense." Speaking of the Messianic prophecies meeting their fulfillment in Christ: " The prophets never thought of making such a combination, nor could such a combination be harmoniously made." The second Psalm " has reference to the reigning king. Whether this king was David or Solomon is immaterial for our present purpose." The twenty-second Psalm " evidently refers to David. Throughout this whole Psalm he describes his own personal feelings and experiences."

" The forty-fifth Psalm, as its title indicates, is a 'song of loves'—that is, a song in celebration of love. It seems to have been a bridal hymn, sung at the marriage of a king." The one hundred and tenth Psalm "was evidently written concerning David by some poet of his time, who would naturally speak of him as his lord." When Christ quoted Ps. 41:9 in Jno. 13:18, "He does not mean to imply that the passage in the Psalm had an original reference to Judas." Although Paul applied the sixty-ninth Psalm to Christ, "from beginning to end of the Psalm there is not the slightest allusion to Christ or to any person other than the Psalmist." When Peter quoted the sixteenth Psalm in Acts 2:27, "there is no evidence whatever to indicate that the doctrine of the resurrection was conceived in David's day. This fact Peter must have known. Hence he could not have imagined that the passage taught the resurrection of the Messiah."

And so on *ad infinitum*, we might almost say, until the head is weary of the contemplation, and "the whole heart faint," if one entertains an expectation of salvation and heaven through the Word of the Living God.

The Messianic Psalms predict, typically and prophetically the Advent, Life, Character, Sufferings and Glory of Jesus Christ. Also His Kingdom and His Salvation for Israel and the Nations. They are Psalms pervaded with the hope of better times for all mankind. This hope entered into the very warp and woof of the Hebrew life, and King David gave it the fullest expression. The following are some of these Psalms: 2, 8, 16, 22, 24, 40, 45, 68, 72, 95,

100, 109, 110, 116, 118. The Highest Critics bear the following testimony to the Messianic import of these and other Psalms: In Matt. 13:35, it is declared that the prophecy in Psalms 78:2, was fulfilled in the teachings of Jesus. Psalm 118:26 is certainly a prophecy of Jesus. See Matt. 21:9, and John 12:13. In Matt. 21:16, Jesus interprets Psalm 8:2 as true of His ministry. In Matt. 22:44; Mark 12:36; and, Luke 20:42, 43, Jesus, as we have seen, declares that Psalm 110:1, refers to Himself. The prophecy in Psalm 22:18, was fulfilled in the casting of "lots" for the Saviour's garments. See Matt. 27:35 and John 19:24. His last words as recorded in Matt. 27:46 and parallels, are recorded in Psalm 22:1. Psalm 31:5, is applied by Jesus to Himself. See Luke 23:46. "Hath not the Scripture said that the Christ cometh of the seed of David." (John 7:42.) Psalms 89:3, 4, and 132:11, are the Scriptures referred to. Jesus said, "But that the Scripture may be fulfilled, he that eateth my bread lifteth up his heel against me." The Scripture Jesus here quotes as true of His betrayer is Psalm 41:9. Jesus said: "But this cometh to pass, that the word may be fulfilled that is written in their law. They hated me without a cause." He quoted Psalms 35:19; 69:4; and, 109:3, and applied them to Himself. Jesus, while on the cross, "That the Scripture might be accomplished, saith, 'I thirst'" (John 19:28.) The Scripture to which He referred is Psalm 69:21. This is most striking! He was in the unutterable agony of His dying hour, and yet He remembers this apparently insignificant prophecy of Himself, and arrests the ebbings of His life, in order that it might be fulfilled. After His resurrection, in His conversation with the two whom he met on the "way to Emmaus," "Beginning from Moses and from all the prophets, He interpreted to them in all the Scriptures the things concerning Himself." Luke 24: 27. The Psalms are a portion of "All the Scriptures;" hence they must have a Messianic import. But He made this very certain, as a little later on He said to the disciples: "These are my words which I spake unto you, while I was yet with you, how that all things must needs be fulfilled, which are written in the law of Moses, and the prophets, and the Psalms, concerning me." Luke 24: 44. And yet many of these critics deny that the Psalms contain any Messianic prophecy. Such denial is a flat contradiction of the above explicit statement of the Son of God.

In Acts 2: 25-32; 13: 35 and 1 Cor. xv: 3, 4 we have incontestable proof that Psalm 16: 8-11 is prophetical of the death and resurrection of our Lord and Saviour.

Peter declared to the "Rulers and elders, and scribes," that Jesus Christ "Is the stone" of which the Psalmist prophetically speaks in Psalm 118: 22, 23. See Acts 4: 11 and 1 Peter 2: 7. Paul in speaking of Jesus, in the synagogue at Antioch, said: "And we bring you good tidings of the promise made unto the fathers, how that God hath fulfilled the same unto our children, in that he raised up Jesus; as also it is written in the second Psalm. Thou art my Son, this day have I begotten Thee." Acts 13: 32, 33. The same testimony is borne in Heb. 1: 5; and v: 5. In Acts 17: 31 it is declared that God "Hath appointed a day, in which He will judge the world in righteousness by the man whom He hath ordained." All this is set forth in Psalm 96: 13. We find in Rom. xv: 3 these words: "For Christ also pleased not Himself; but as it is written, The reproaches of them that reproached Thee fell upon Me." Where is this written? In Psalm 69: 9. The declaration made in 1 Cor. xv: 25–27, is but the echo of Psalms 2: 6–10; 8: 6; 45: 3, 6, and 110: 1. "Wherefore he saith" (of Christ); and Psalm 68: 18 is then quoted (see Eph. 4: 8). Speaking of Jesus the Christ, in Hebrews 1: 6–9, the inspired penman quotes Psalms 97: 7 and 45: 6, 7, as fulfilled in connection with the advent of our Lord. In Heb. 2: 12, Psalm 22: 22, is applied to Jesus Christ. In Heb. v: 6, 10 and 7: 17, 21, it is declared that Psalm 110: 4 is true of Jesus Christ. Psalm 40: 6–8, was fulfilled in Jesus as we learn in Heb. x: 5–7. Rev. 2: 27 and 19: 15 identifies Jesus with the prophecy of Psalm 2: 9. Rev. xv: 4 makes it certain that Christ was prophetically referred to in Psalm 86: 9. The prophecy in Psalm 45: 3, 4, without doubt refers to the Messiah in Kingly glory. See Rev. 19: 11.

And so we see that the Highest Critics again and again, in most explicit terms and unmistakable language utterly refute the views and opinions of the

Higher Critics, that none of the Psalms are Messianic in their prophetical outlook. I am sure that the millions who have felt the thrill of these divine harmonies, and believe that Jesus Christ, the Holy Spirit and the Apostles were competent to express an opinion upon the matters under discussion; that they did not lie, or were not duped, but did tell the truth, will not hesitate for one moment in deciding whom to believe. "Let God be true and every man a liar."

In face of this unbelieving criticism, and in face of swerving loyalty of scholars from whom better things were to be expected, we hold to the testimony of the Highest Critics. Were it necessary it could be supported by the testimony of the Jewish Church who referred to the Messiah in the very Psalms to which I have called attention. We could quote from standard translations of Talmud and Targum alike, but it is unnecessary. The inner witness of the Sacred Books themselves, the fulfillment of the Psalms in the person of Christ, and the hope of Messianic glory common to both Jews and Gentiles, proved that David spoke by the Spirit (2 Sam. 23:2), was a "Seer" as well as a "Prophet," and foretold "The sufferings of Christ, and the glory that should follow" (1 Peter 1:10, 11).

The Psalmody of Israel broke out where David was enthroned. It broke out again in Isaiah's time, when Judah was delivered from the Assyrian yoke, and again when Judah returned from Babylonian exile. It is here belong the "Songs of Degrees"—

the music of the Pilgrims marching to Zion. Psalms were written during the various invasions of Judah by Heathen nations; also when the Chaldeans destroyed the city and burned the Temple; also during the captivity, and during the restoration. From Moses to Ezra the stream of song was perpetuated in the solemn liturgy of the chosen race, bursting upward in floods of ebullient emotion and Messianic praise. It sounded not only the glories of the Messianic King to come, but breathed the sorrows that precede his enthronement. It poured forth the penitential confession of sin, and the jubilant expressions of gratitude for divine forgiveness. There is not a chord of religious experience, or a faith or hope it did not touch. And King David, the sweet singer of Israel, though others also sang sweet songs, was the master hand in all. The false criticism that would assign some of the noblest of these productions to Maccabean times, in honor of the exploits of Maccabean princes, or their transient independence, or as utterances of distress in times of Syrian persecution, is repelled by the fact that the Psalter, in its five-fold arrangement, was known as early as the times of the Chronicles, *i. e.*, in the fourth century before Christ.

Christ in His sufferings and Christ in His glory is the substance and sense of all Israel's Prophecy, of all Israel's Psalmody, of all Israel's History. He is the end of the Prophets, and the Psalms, just as He is the end of the Law, and of History. May the Lord smite the criticism that teaches otherwise!

Christ, and Christ alone, is the key that unlocks the entire Old Testament. When Philip showed this to the Assyrian State Minister, the Ethiopian rode in his chariot "rejoicing." Had Philip been a Higher Critic "Queen Candace's prime-minister had worn a blacker face! Had Peter been a Higher Critic the scenes at Pentecost had never occurred. Had Jesus been a Higher Critic—in the sense of modern Higher Critics —-the gloom had never been lifted from the hearts of the wanderers to Emmaus on the afternoon of the first Christian Sabbath! "The key of David," said Hilary, "is the Person of Jesus."

CHAPTER XIII.

ISAIAH.

The Higher Critics subject the Bible to what they call "Literary" and "Historical tests." This is all right, providing the tests are all right. Sometimes they are; oftentimes they are not, since they are based upon human opinion, which, too often, is biased, and never infallible. Therefore, the working rules of these gentlemen are usually but postulates. The mischief done by the rationalistically disposed comes of their eliminating the supernatural from their rules. Doing this, they are compelled to deny that a prophet was in any sense a seer and foreteller, except within the limits of his own time. Just here these Critics work the theory they call "Time Historical," or "Near Horizon." The theory is thus stated by two of them:

"The prophets were bounded like other men by the horizon of their own views, and occupied themselves only with that future whose rewards and punishments were likely to reach their contemporaries."

"Isaiah prophesied and predicted all he did from loyalty to two simple truths, which he tells us he received from God Himself—that sin must be punished, and that the people of God must be saved. This simple faith, acting with a wonderful knowledge of human nature and ceaseless vigilance of affairs, constituted inspiration for Isaiah. For the exact conditions and forms, both of the punishment and its relief, the prophets depended upon their own knowledge of the world."

Here is a sample: " In the promise that a virgin shall bring forth a child, Isa. vii: 13-17, 'the natural and original reference is to the birth of a child, which was shortly to take place. Hence there is no direct, much less exclusive, reference here to the Messiah."

Of course this theory brings them into direct conflict with the Highest Critics. But this is not an insuperable difficulty, as we have already seen, for they audaciously and arbitrarily set their testimony aside as incompetent. The Messianic prophecies in this and other books are easily disposed of by insisting that there are none. The chief point of difficulty encountered by them in the Book of Isaiah, is the prophecy concerning Cyrus and his kingdom. They are compelled, by indisputable historical facts, to either confess that Isaiah was a remote foreseer, or deny that he was the author of that part of the Book. This latter is what they have done. They allow that Isaiah wrote chapters one and thirty-nine, inclusive; but, as he could not possibly have seen one hundred and fifty years into the future, some writer, to them unknown, contemporaneous with the times of Cyrus, wrote chapters forty and sixty-six, inclusive. His writings indicate that he was quite the peer of Isaiah, David and Moses, and yet the Jewish nation did not know him. He is referred to one hundred times in the New Testament, but no Apostle or Evangelist can tell who he is. The fact is, he is a creature of the fancy of these gentlemen, created to support their postulates, so that they will work smoothly. That is to say, there is no such personage; there is not the slightest proof of it; he is purely and wholly fictitious, an impostor and idealistic fraud. In order to be consistent they have thrown out the four historical chapters, *i.e.*, thirty-six and thirty-nine inclusive, on the assumed grounds that they, with the exception of the Song of Hezekiah, chap. 38:9-20, and narrating certain important events in which Isaiah was concerned, do not differ verbally, from 2 Kings, 18:13; 18:17-20 and 19. And, as there are prophecies in chapters one and thirty-five, inclusive, that reached beyond the lifetime of Isaiah, they have cut out the chapters containing them; so that now, they allow he wrote twenty-six chapters. At the speed they are now traveling, Isaiah will be left as far behind in a little while, in matters of authorship, by these destructionists, as David and Moses.

The Book of Isaiah has three natural divisions, and seven sub-divisions. The first thirty-five chapters constitute, most naturally, the older prophecies; the last twenty-seven the later. Lying between these are four historical chapters, which relate to the Assyrian invasion of the land, the illness of King Hezekiah and his miraculous restoration to health. The sub-divisions are as follows: *First*—Chapters 1-12, recite the judgments visited upon Judah and Israel. *Second*—Chapters 13-26, contain foreign prophecies and an account of the punishment visited upon seven Gentile nations that oppressed Israel. *Third*—Chapters 27-35, are a sublime apocalypse wherein are additional woes pronounced upon Israel. Each of these three groups ends with a song of praise in view of the second coming of the Lord. *Fourth*—Chapters 36-39, are historical. *Fifth*—Chapters 40-48: we have here "God in creation, chap. 40; God in providence, chap. 41; God in redemption, chap. 42; and God in the deliverance of His people from Babylonian oppression, chap. 43." Cyrus is the middle point of this group, and is the key with which to unlock it. *Sixth*—Chapters 49-57, Jesus Christ as the servant of Jehovah is the central figure in this group, and is represented as the one Great Deliverer from all oppression and servitude. *Seventh*—Chapters 58-66, the millennial age, with the new heavens and the new earth are the prominent things in this group, with restored Jerusalem shining forth as the central figure. Each of these last three sub-divisions ends with this thought: "There is no peace, saith my God to the wicked." The last expressed in different language.

The question of the Prophet being able to see beyond his "Own Horizon" is the one to which the Highest Critics will now testify. The testimony of the Book will be limited to the prophecies concerning Jesus Christ, with only a very few glances at its eschatology. In Isa. 7:14, it is said: "Therefore the Lord Himself shall give you a sign; behold a virgin shall conceive, and bear a son, and shall call

His name Immanuel." In Matt. 1 : 20, 21, we have the fulfillment of this prophecy, recited, for in the twenty-second verse of the same chapter, it is said: "Now all this is come to pass, that it might be fulfilled which was spoken by the Lord through the Prophet saying"—and then the twenty-third verse is a quotation of Isa. 7 : 14. Luke 2 : 11, and John 3 : 16, tell us that Isa. 9 : 6 was fulfilled in the birth and gift of Jesus Christ. Without doubt the manifestation of Jesus Christ, at the "Day of the Lord," is declared in Isa. 10 : 17. See 2 Thess. 2 : 7–9, and Heb. 12 : 29. In Isa. 11 : 1, 10, we have an explicit prophecy that Jesus " shall come forth * * * out of the stock of Jesse." "That the root of Jesse," etc., etc. Of course this prophecy could not possibly refer to King David, as he had been dead more than three hundred years when it was uttered. That it referred to Jesus, Acts 13 : 22, 23, clearly teaches. Matt. 28 : 18, John 10 : 11–16, and 1 John 3 : 8 make it sure that our Lord Jesus Christ is the person meant in Isa. 40 : 10, 11. Do not Luke 2 : 32 and Acts 13 : 47 teach clearly that Isa. 49 : 6 (last clause) is a prophecy of Jesus the Christ?

The fifty-third chapter of Isaiah is, from first to last, distinctively and particularly Messianic. How any honest man professing to believe that the Bible is God's Word, or even that it contains God's Word, with the fifty-third chapter of Isaiah before him, can say "It contains no Messianic import whatever," is impossible for me to understand. But, let us glance at it verse by verse:

Verse 1.—Who hath believed our report? and to whom hath the arm of the Lord been revealed?

"Yet they believed not on Him: that the word of Isaiah the prophet might be fulfilled, which he spake, "Lord who hath believed our report? and to whom hath the arm of the Lord been revealed?" John 12:37, 38.

Verse 2.—There is no beauty that we should desire Him.

"But they cried out all together, saying: "Away with this man." Luke 23:18.

Verse 3.—A man of sorrows and acquainted with grief.

"Then said He unto them, My soul is exceeding sorrowful, even unto death." Matt. 26:38.

Verse 4.—Surely He hath borne our griefs (Heb., sicknesses) and carried our sorrows.

"That it might be fulfilled which was spoken by Isaiah the prophet, saying, Himself took our infirmities and bore our diseases." Matt. 8:17.

Verse 5.—The chastisement of our peace was upon Him.

"Having made peace through the blood of His cross." Col. 1:20.

Verse 6.—The Lord hath laid on Him the iniquity of us all.

"Who His own self bore our sins in His body upon the tree." 1 Peter 2:24.

Verse 7.—As a sheep that before her shearers is dumb; yea, he opened not His mouth.

"And the eunuch answered Philip, and said, I pray thee, of whom speaketh the prophet this? of Himself or of some other? And Philip opened his mouth, and beginning from this Scripture preached unto him Jesus." Acts 8:32-35.

Verse 8.—For the transgression of my people was He stricken.

"Him who knew no sin He made to be sin on our behalf." 2 Cor. 5:21,

Verse 9.—And they made his grave with the wicked, and with the rich in his death.

"And when even was come, there came a rich man * * * and asked for the body of Jesus * * * and laid it in his own new tomb." Matt. 27 : 57-60.

Verse 10.—He hath put Him to grief.

"Having become a curse for us." Gal. 3 : 13. Thou shalt make His soul an offering for sin.
"He was manifested to take away sins." 1 John 3 : 5.

Verse 11.—He shall see the travail of His soul and shall be satisfied.

"For Christ is the end of the law for righteousness to every one that believeth." Rom. 10 : 4.
By His knowledge shall my righteous servant justify many.
"Justified freely by His grace through the redemption that is in Christ Jesus." Rom. 3 : 24.

Verse 12.—Therefore will I divide Him a portion with the great, and he shall divide the spoil with the strong.
"That through death He might bring to naught him that had the power of death, that is the devil; and might deliver all them who through fear of death were all their lifetime subject to bondage." Heb. 2 : 14, 15.
And was numbered with the transgressors.
"There they crucified Him, and the malefactors, one on the right hand and the other on the left." Luke 23-33.
And made intercession for the transgressors.
"He ever liveth to make intercession for them." Heb. 7 : 25.
"If any man sin, we have an Advocate with the Father, Jesus Christ, the righteous." 1 John 2 : 1.

Romans 11 : 26 tells us explicitly that Isa. 59 : 20 is prophetical of Jesus Christ.

In Luke 4 : 16-19 Jesus Christ quotes Isa. 61 : 1 and half of 2 ; and, in the twenty-first verse, He says: "To-day hath this Scripture been fulfilled in your ears." John 1 : 32; Acts 10 : 38 ; and Heb. 1 : 9, surely teach that the first part of the first verse of sixty-first chapter of Isaiah is prophetical of Jesus. Heb. 7 : 25 tells us that the "Mighty to save," of Isa. 63 : 1, is Jesus the Christ. And thus from beginning to end we see the Messiah as Saviour and King—in humiliation and glory. To deny the prophetical characteristics of this Book, is to deny the plainest teachings of the Word of God.

The unity of the Book is plainly discernible in the faultless symmetry of the whole. Even from the "Literary Tests," of the Higher Critics, this is easily and most certainly deducible. Put on your literary spectacles. It will do you no harm to wear them if the Holy Spirit has enlightened the eyes of your understanding. Reading carefully you must be struck by the very great similarity of styles between the two portions of the book. Such expressions as: "The mouth of the Lord has spoken;" "Drunken, but not with wine ;" "The lion shall eat straw like the ox;" "Wilderness blossoming;" "The Holy one of Israel," etc., are repeatedly found. Prof. Delitzsch calls attention to the frequent interchange of the name of Jacob with Israel in both parts of the book; and, the sententiousness of expression and same breathless haste in the movement of thought, everywhere discernible. Who, competent to judge, can doubt that the 35th chapter is the prelude to the majestic harmonies in the 40th and 66th chapters inclusive.

The entire Book of Isaiah was attributed to the Son of Amoz by the Great Synagogue, composed of such illustrious men as Ezra, Nehemiah, Zachariah and Haggai, nearly five hundred years before Christ. If the theory of a Deutero-Isaiah is true would not these great and learned men have known it? They knew nothing of any one but the Proto and only Isaiah.

The Septuagint, or Greek version of the Old Testament, which was begun nearly three hundred years before Christ, recognizes but one Isaiah for the entire Book.

The Talmud and Targums ascribe the Book, as such, to Isaiah. The Critics are significantly silent in regard to the valuable testimony of these ancient and much venerated writings, on this question.

The later Synagogue knew nothing of a Deutero-Isaiah. They used the Book every Sabbath day as the Book of Isaiah, and thirteen out of its sixteen prophetic readings were taken from chapters 40–66.

Isaiah is referred to in Ecclesiasticus, where it is written that "in his time the sun went backward and he lengthened the king's life. He saw by an excellent spirit what should come at the last and he comforted them that mourned in Sion, he showed what should come to pass forever, and secret things or ever they came." A reference which shows that the writer of that book believed that the Isaiah of King Hezekiah's reign was also he who wrote the later prophecies of the book.

The author of the first part of the book wrote in the reign of Hezekiah (see Isaiah 1 : 1) and the author of the second part of the book speaks of Hezekiah's wife as a type of restored Israel. See Isaiah 62 : 4 and 2 Kings 21 : 1.

John the Baptist said Isaiah wrote the third, fourth and fifth verses of the fortieth chapter of the book bearing his name. Hear him: "I am the voice of one crying in the wilderness, make straight the way of the Lord, as said Isaiah the prophet." John 1 : 23. See also, Luke 3 : 3-6. The Higher Critics teach that this unequivocal testimony of the Baptist is false.

The four evangelists and apostles believed the one great prophet to be the writer of the entire book, and quote 125 verses from it and refer to the whole book 162 times.

The following testimonies explicitly declare that Isaiah was the author of portions (and if portions, then the whole) of chapters 40-66—" That it might be fulfilled which was spoken by Isaiah the prophet, saying"—And then the inspired penman quotes Isa. 53 : 4. See Matt. 8 : 17. " That it might be fulfilled which was spoken by Isaiah, the prophet, saying"—And then Isa. 42 : 1-3, is quoted. Matt. 12 : 17. "And there was delivered unto Him (Jesus the Christ) the book of the prophet Isaiah, and he opened the book, and found the place where it was written," and then read the first verse and the first half of the second of the sixty-first chapter. Let it be observed that the portion read was in the sixty-first chapter; and the book was "The book of the prophet Isaiah." "That the word of Isaiah the prophet might be fulfilled which he spake." This word is found in Isa. 53: 1, and is quoted. John 12: 38–40.

Luke, writing by inspiration of the Holy Spirit says: "And Philip ran to him, and heard him reading Isaiah the prophet. * * * Now the place of the Scripture which he was reading was—" And then he quotes Isa. 53: 7, 8. See Acts 8: 30–33.

Paul, under Divine guidance, says: "For Isaiah saith," and then he quotes the first clause of the first verse of the fifty-first chapter. See Rom. 10: 16. And again: "And Isaiah is very bold and saith—" and then he quotes Isa. 65: 1. See Rom. 10: 20.

The Jewish Church never entertained any other thought of the authorship than the Proto-Isaiah; and the consensus of the Christian Church from the first has been this: Isaiah wrote the entire prophecy of Isaiah.

Josephus (Antiq. 9, 13, 3) speaks of Isaiah the prophet as one who lived in the days of Hezekiah (also Antiq. 10, 1, 3). Then (Antiq. 11, 1, 2) he gives the remarkable story of Cyrus bringing help to the people, the reason for his conduct being "his reading the book which Isaiah left behind him of his prophecies." Josephus adds, "This was foretold by Isaiah one hundred and forty years before the Temple was demolished." It is certainly to be regretted that the advocates of the new criticism fail to deal with this ancient historical testimony to the single authorship.

The wording of the decree of Cyrus ordering the erection of the temple of Jerusalem, is taken from that part of the prophecy written, as the Higher Critics tell us, after the day of Cyrus.

There is no way to deny that such a decree was issued except by declaring the whole book of Ezra to be a lie, for when the work of rebuilding the temple was interrupted, and Darius was on the throne, "There was found at Achmetha, in the palace that is in the province of the Medes, a roll, and therein was a record thus written: In the first year of Cyrus the king, the same Cyrus the king made a decree concerning the house of God at Jerusalem, Let the house be builded, the place where they offer sacrifices." Ezra vi: 2, 3.

Here is the decree: "Thus saith Cyrus king of Persia. The Lord God of heaven hath given me all the kingdoms of the earth; and He hath charged me to build Him an house at Jerusalem, which is in Judah. Who is there among you of all His people? his God be with him, and let him go up to Jerusalem, which is in Judah, and build the house of the Lord God of Israel (He is the God), which is in Jerusalem," Ez. i: 2, 3.

Here is the prophecy: "That saith of Cyrus, *He is* my shepherd, and shall perform all my pleasure: even saying of Jerusalem, She shall be built; and to the temple, Thy foundation shall be laid.

Thus saith the LORD to his annointed, to Cyrus, whose right hand I have holden, to subdue nations before him, and I will loose the loins of kings; to open the doors before him, and the gates shall not be shut; I will go before thee, and make the rugged places plain: I will break in pieces the doors of brass, and cut in sunder the bars of iron: and I will give thee the treasures of darkness, and hidden riches of secret places, that thou mayest know that I am the LORD, which call thee by thy name, even the God of Israel. For Jacob my servant's sake, and Israel my chosen, I have called thee by thy name: I have surnamed thee, though thou hast not known me. I am the LORD, and there is none else; beside me there is no God: I will gird thee, though thou hast not known me." Isa. 44:28; 45:1-5.

It is here stated (1) that a prophecy concerning Cyrus and the rebuilding of the Temple was uttered; (2) that Cyrus promulgated a decree in accordance with the prophecy; and (3) we find the prophecy in the Book of Isaiah. Now, then, the question is simply this: Who wrote the prophecy? The Higher Critics say Isaiah did not, because a prophet could not possibly see one hundred and fifty years into the future; and our "Literary Tests" show a different style of composition in chapters 40-66, from what we find in chapters 1-39. The first postulate is audacious and eliminates the supernatural from inspiration; and the second arbitrarily requires a man to have exactly the same style of composition at sixty years of age as he had at twenty-five; and rules that it is impossible for any one to have more than one style of writing.

Josephus says Isaiah wrote it. To this agree the Septuagint version, the Talmud, the Targums, the Great Synagogue, the later Synagogue, Ecclesiasticus, John the Baptist, Jesus, the Holy Spirit speaking by Matthew, Luke, John and Paul, and the Church, both Jewish and Christian, in all ages. And there is absolutely not one demonstrable fact to the contrary.

If an other than the son of Amoz wrote chapters 40–66, where are his credentials? Isaiah began his message by saying, "Hear the word of the Lord," and thus "saith the Lord." Isa. 1: 10, 11. Nearly all the prophets of God say the same thing. But no such announcement is made in the opening of the section embraced in chapters 40-66. Is it at all reasonable to conclude that the mighty monarch Cyrus could be duped by an unknown person into rebuilding the Temple, a most stupendous and costly undertaking? Surely he knew it was the will of God that he should do this great work; and most surely he knew the prophecy came by a prophet properly accredited, who lived long before his day, even Isaiah, the son of Amoz.

I say with Dr. Joseph Addison Alexander, of Princeton, who, to use the admission of Dr. Philip Schaff: "Handled the Higher Critics without gloves,"—"That the criticism we are called to respect, destroys the inspiration of the Scriptures, and rests on assumptions as arbitrary and capricious as the adventurous spirits who conceived them."

CHAPTER XIV.

DANIEL.

The narrative of this Book is very much disconnected. History and prophecy, incidents, dreams and visions are so interwoven that it stands unique among the prophecies of the Old Testament. And yet it is very naturally divided. The first six chapters are historical, while the last six are predictive. In the historical part, though it is not wholly historical, as it contains a few predictions, we find that Daniel and his three companions were taken from Jerusalem after its capture by Nebuchadnezzar, to the royal court in Babylon; and numerous events that occurred during the reigns of Nebuchadnezzar, Darius and Cyrus are accurately recorded, as is shown by profane history, and very clearly proven by cuneiform texts that archæologists have recently brought to light. The predictive portion, though it is in part historical, relates chiefly to the Babylonian, Medo-Persian, Macedonian and Roman kingdoms. There can be no reasonable doubt raised against the fact that the four kingdoms in chapter two and the four beasts in chapter seven are the same, and signify the four above mentioned kingdoms. Porphyry acknowledged that these prophecies were literally fulfilled, though he insisted that they must have been written after the events! These last six chapters are not limited, predictively, **to** these four kingdoms and to Antiochus Epiphanes, but are in a large sense Messianic and eschatological, as we shall see a little further on.

In the Jewish Canon of the Old Testament this Book was not found among the prophets but in the miscellaneous writings called the *Hagiographa*. This fact, together with the fact that the writing does not begin, as do the other prophecies, with the declaration that it is "The Word of the Lord," is used by the Critics to justify them in discrediting it as of equal authority with the others. But the Psalms of David are also included in the *Hagiographa* and do not begin with such declaration, as are also Job, Proverbs, Canticles, Ruth, Ezra, Chronicles, Ecclesiastes and Esther. Shall we discredit all these? We must if the presence of a Book in the third collection of the Sacred Writings justifies it.

After his return from exile, Daniel was commanded to "seal up" his Apocalypse "Unto the time of the end," *i. e.*, not to expose it to public reading and use, for the time of the event predicted as occurring after the release was not at hand. The events related to the distant future, viz.: to the End-time of the third prophetic Empire, or time of the Syrian Antichrist, and to the End-time of the fourth prophetic Empire, or the time of the last Antichrist. Perhaps this order to seal the Book and keep it from public use was a reason why the Book of Daniel was not put among the prophetic Books by Ezra and the compilers of the Jewish Canon; and Daniel's name not enumerated among the names of the prophets. Perhaps, also, it was a reason why when the End-time of the Greek Empire came, and Antiochus Epiphanes raged against the people of God, it was produced by the High Priests and Custodians of the Sacred Oracles, and was so popular. Perhaps, also, it was again the very reason why our Lord refers to "Daniel the Prophet" lest any might suppose he was not a prophet, because his Book was not among the prophetic Books, but in the "Other Writings."

While it is true Daniel's Prophecy is not introduced, as are nearly all the other prophecies, by the statement that it is the Lord who is speaking, yet it is true that Daniel uttered the words of the Lord, for in chapter 10:9, he says: "Yet heard I the voice of His words: and when I heard the voice of His words;" so that his revelation is as certainly from the Lord as any other of the Prophets.

But many of the same critics deny that other of the prophecies are "The Words of the Lord," even where they are introduced by this statement. So their chief effort is, apparently, to find objections to the writing, rather than to ascertain by what authority and to what intent were these books written.

THE AUTHORSHIP.

The Higher Critics insist that Daniel had nothing whatever to do with the authorship of this Book. They fail utterly, however, to explain how it ever came to be called "The Book of Daniel;" nor, can they tell us who is the author. They find refuge in that most illustrious literary family the world ever knew, *i. e.*, The Unknown.

They insist that it was written some time between 300 B. C., and the times of Antiochus Epiphanes; the more rationalistic among them insisting that the work was done during the year 167 B. C. They reach this conclusion, inevitably, because their "Near Horizon" theory will not allow the prophet to see beyond his own times, and, because they studied eschatology in the school of conjecture, which school is located in the State of Don't-know-dom; and the prophetic truth of Daniel as to the Anti-Christ, is sacrificed upon the altar of a Pre-Christ called Antiochus Epiphanes.

It is not possible that a writer living at so late a date as 167 B. C., could delineate so accurately the details of the historic narratives of this Book, as the cuneiform records prove them to be. These cuneiform records have verified almost every historic statement of the Book, and disclosed no error anywhere, which fact is inconceivable from the standpoint of authorship assumed by the Critics. Francois Lenormant, Prof. of Archæology at the National Library of France, says: "The more often I read the Book of Daniel and compare it with the cuneiform records, the more striking seems the fidelity of the picture given by the first six chapters of the Babylonian court, and the superstitions of the time of Nebuchadnezzar, and the more strongly am I impressed with the conviction that at least this portion of the Book was written in Babylon itself, and not far from the time of the events related, and so the more impracticable and incorrect it seems to me to transfer its origin to a date as late as that of Antiochus Epiphanes."

The first six chapters of the Book of Daniel have a historical value which cannot be contested, confirmed as it is by the recovered cuneiform texts. They must, therefore, have been composed at a date not far removed from the persons and events of which they treat, by some one having access to the original Babylonian documents, perhaps fragments of Nebuchadnezzar's official annals.

The style, temper, sentiment, movement of thought and personal characteristics of this writing belong to a much earlier time than 300 B. C. Even Canon Driver admits that "In warmth of religious feeling, and in the unflinching maintenance of Divine truth, the Book resembles closely enough the writings of the older prophets."

Dr. Pusey says: "I would note, how Dr. Payne Smith, Mr. McGill and myself, independently of one another, observed that Daniel and Ezra agree so remarkably, not only in differing from the Targums, but in their correspondence with Western Aramaic or Syriac. This correspondence, too, belongs very remarkably to the grammar as well as to the vocabulary. This is further illustrated by the correspondence with what Mr. McGill rightly calls the "Syrizing" Targums. This character of the Chaldee, of Daniel and Ezra separates them off from the Targums, which come nearest to their age, by an almost dialectic difference, analagous to the difference of the Greek of Homer from that of later Greek writers, when the dialects became distinct. It is yet further illustrated by the correspondence of both Daniel and Ezra with the Samaritan, which, whatever be the age of its Targum, was separated off from its parent-stock of Eastern Aramaic at a period earlier than even Daniel and Ezra."

Perowne says: "The use of the Aryan words chiefly turns the scale on the side of the earlier date."

Josephus tells us that Alexander the Great entered Jerusalem about 330 B. C., and offered sacrifice to God in the Temple, where the High Priest showed him the prophecies of Daniel (Dan. 7:6; 8:7) which predicted the overthrow of the Persian Empire by a Greek King, which he felt could apply to none other than himself.

The Talmud tells us that the Book of Daniel dates from the time of the Great Synagogue. If it only dates from 167 B. C., on what grounds can its presence in the Septuagint version be accounted for, without arbitrarily denying the incontestable evidence of the age of this venerable document?

Canon Driver says: "Jesus, the son of Sirach (writing 200 B. C)., in his enumeration of Israelitish worthies, chaps. 44-50, though he mentions Isaiah, Jeremiah, Ezekiel and (collectively) the Twelve Minor Prophets, is silent as to Daniel."

The following answer is taken from Smith's Bible Dictionary: "In reply to these remarks, it may be urged, that if the Book of Daniel was already placed among the *Hagiographa* at the time when the " Wisdom of Sirach " was written, the omission of the name of Daniel (Eccles. 49) is most natural, and that under any circumstances the omission is not more remarkable than that of Ezra and the twelve lesser prophets, for 49 : 10 is probably an interpolation intended to supply a supposed defect."

And so the Canon—as other critics—in his desperate straits to find arguments that will support his non-prophetic view of this Book, tries to prove his position by the use of a probably interpolated passage from a secular writing.

Daniel is mentioned repeatedly in the Book as its author. See chapters 7 : 2, 15, 28 ; 8 : 1 ; 9: 22; 10: 1–19 ; 12 : 5. In the first six chapters Daniel speaks of himself in the third person. In Chapter 6 he speaks in the first person : " I, Daniel, etc.," and claims to have received a revelation from heaven. This is no proof that there were two authors. Cæsar, Thucydides and others spoke of themselves in the third person as well as in the first. It was a common practice in ancient times. Moreover, in the last six chapters, Daniel, who speaks of himself in the first person, speaks of himself twice in the third person. See Dan. 7 : 1 ; 10: 1. The entire cast and setting of the work is altogether consistent with his authorship.

Matt. 24 : 15 tells us that Jesus said : " When therefore ye see the abomination of desolation which was spoken of by Daniel the prophet," etc.,

etc. We here note that Jesus said Dan. 9: 26, 27 was spoken by Daniel; and, notwithstanding the critics have removed him from the illustrious company of the holy prophets, Jesus most explicitly states that he was one, and uttered at least one prediction that has a clear and distinct eschatological significance. This testimony of the Highest Critic settles not only the question of authorship but of the age of the Book as well. To question this testimony is to degrade the son of God to the level of the Higher Critics and rob Him of His Godhood. Such questioning makes the teachings of Jesus the Christ of no greater value than those of Socrates, Edmund Burk or Renan; and places us, as touching the purposes of God in grace, on a stormy sea, in an open boat without rudder, chart or compass. It is destructive to the last degree, and should be most emphatically condemned by all who profess loyalty to God's word and the teachings of Jesus Christ the Saviour of men.

The Critics insist upon a dual authorship, because the Book is divided into two parts, according to their "Literary Tests," though many competent Critics such as Hitzig and DeWette, think otherwise. They—the Critics—call attention to the fact that about half the Book is written in Hebrew and the other half in Aramaic, as though this fact supported their theory. But they met with an insuperable difficulty in the fact that the first chapter is in Hebrew and the seventh in Aramaic.

They question the historical accuracy of the first

six chapters on the ground of the many extraordinary miracles recorded therein. If they were to apply this rule to the four Gospels, the world would be left almost wholly without any historical knowledge of Jesus the Christ.

The dimensions of the golden image which Nebuchadnezzar caused to be erected on the plain of Dura are said, by the Critics, to be without doubt, an exaggeration. They reason from this assumption that the Book, historically, is therefore unreliable, and, to be consistent, not inspired at all. Prof. Lenormant says " That it was the custom to erect golden images of colossal size, admits of no question. The three statues which crowned the pyramid E-saggal in Babylon, previous to its sacking by Xerxes, represented (according to Diodorus Siculus) together with their altar and other appurtenances, a weight of gold of 5,850 talents, 143,559 kilogrammes —*i. e.*, a value of 430,677,000 francs. The sanctuary of the storied pyramid at Borsippa contained (at least up to the time of Xerxes) a similar massive golden image, the height of which was, according to Herodotus not less than twelve cubits."

Prof. Pusey says: "I am indebted for my knowledge of the following facts to my friend Dr. Greenhill: 'The Marquis de Beauvoir thus describes the pagoda of Xetuphon. Imagine yourself with us beneath a colonnade of teak-wood, and in an immense sanctuary, where the god is extended his full length; and this is no small matter, for he measured one hundred and fifty feet from the shoulder to the soles of his feet. This gigantic body, in masonry, is completely and entirely guilt. It lies on the right side; a guilded terrace, ornamented with sculptures. serves for his couch. His head, of which the summit is eighty feet above the ground, is supported by the right arm, which rests towards the entrance door. His left arm is extended along the thigh; his eyes are of silver, his lips pink enamel, and on his head is a crown of red gold. We look like Lilliputians around Gulliver; and if we try to climb up upon him, we disappear altogether in his nostrils: one of his nails is taller than any of us. We stood amazed before this Titian work, of which the architect can only have been paid by the riches of Crœsus. This gigantic coating of the purest gold must be worth Milliards; each sheet of metal (and there must have been thousands) is nearly two square feet in size, and weighs, they tell us, 450 ounces of gold."

"Another Buddha, in the royal Pagoda, of ordinary dimensions, is of massive gold; its head is of a single emerald, delicately cut and of a marvelous luster, surmounted with a helmet of sapphire and opal. The English Consul is said to have offered for it a million pounds sterling in the name of his government. The annals of the kingdom speak of its discovery seven or eight centuries ago."

And so we know that others in those far east countries besides Nebuchadnezzar were given to the pastime or religious duty of manufacturing colossal golden images, and thus verifying Daniel's story.

THE PROPHESIES OF THE BOOK.

Nebuchadnezzar's dream of the great image and the increasing stone was accurately interpreted by Daniel. The Babylonian Kingdom was indicated by the "Head of gold;" the Medo-Persian by the "breast and arms of silver;" the Macedonian, or Grecian, by the "Belly and thighs (sides) of brass;" the Roman by the "Legs of iron;" and the ten sub-divisions of the Roman Empire by the "Ten toes of iron and clay." The predictive teaching of this image and the interpretation of it by Daniel, has been demonstrated by history, in that the things foreseen and foretold have most surely come to pass. The efforts of the Higher Critics to destroy the prophetical characteristics of this Book are pitiable in the extreme, and certainly ought to be humiliating to all honest and reverent scholars.

It was quite as much a prophecy to describe the world-wide Empire of Rome 167 years B. C., as it would have been to do so 600 years B. C., and in their efforts to reconcile the facts in the case to their theory, the Higher Critics invaribly beg the question or throw dust into the air.

Concerning the interpretation given of "The Stone" (See Dan. 2; 35, 44, 45), it may here be said, it is not possible, by any established ruler of interpretation and exegesis, to reconcile it to the fact historically recorded of any kingdom the world has yet seen. "The Stone" represented a Kingdom that shall subdue, overthrow and destroy all other kingdoms, becoming universal and to "stand forever." There is nothing, historically nothing, prospectively nothing, and conjecturally nothing, that will answer to the interpretation, save the Messianic Kingdom; and this does, in every particular. See Psa. 2: 6–9; Luke 1: 31–33; Rev. 11: 15; Phil. 2: 9–11; etc., etc.

In chapter seven we have a record of "A dream and visions" that Daniel had, which were prophetical of the same things predicted in Nebuchadnezzar's dream, excepting—as we shall see—apocalyptically, they were more comprehensive and specific. In this case Babylon is represented by a "Lion," Medo-Persia by a "Bear," Greece by a "Leopard," Rome by "A fourth beast," and the ten kingdoms by the "Ten horns of the 'Fourth beast.'" From among the "Ten horns" arises a "Little horn," and it becomes mightier than all the rest. It cannot possibly be Antiochus Epiphanes, because it was not manifested until after the destruction of the Roman Empire; and, it is itself the mighty power that uproots three of the ten-horn kingdoms, and subdues the other seven, the ten arising out of the Roman Empire. These kingdoms still exist, and the prophecy plainly tells us that the "Little horn's" power is to be manifested in the end times of this dispensation. Let us analyze the chapter and see what it teaches about the "Little horn:"

First—It appears in the end time. Verses 21, 22.
Second—It usurps Divine prerogatives. Verses 24, 25.
Third—It has the power of blasphemy. Verse 25.
Fourth—It persecutes the Saints. Verse 25.
Fifth—It comes to its end suddenly. Verse 11.

Sixth—It goes into perdition. Verses 11, 26.

Seventh—Its destruction, the coming of the Lord, the gathering together of the Saints and the establishing of the everlasting kingdom synchronize. Verses 13, 14, 18, 27.

Will the reader now please turn to 2 Thess. 2: 1–9 and let us see what are the characteristics of the "Man of Sin," and what of his future:

First—He appears in the end time. Verses 2 and 3.
Second—He is energized by Satan. Verse 9.
Third—He usurps Divine prerogatives. Verse 4.
Fourth—He is a blasphemer. Verse 4.
Fifth—He possesses superhuman power. Verse 9.
Sixth—He persecutes the Saints and many fall away. Verse 3.
Seventh—He comes to his end suddenly. Verse 8.
Eighth—He goes into perdition. Verse 3.
Ninth—The coming of the Lord and gathering of the Saints synchronize with his destruction. Verse 8.

Now will the reader please turn to Revelation, chapter thirteen, and notice the characteristics of "The Beast" with the wounded head:

First—He is energized by Satan. Verses 2 and 4.
Second—He is a great world power. Verse 7.
Third—He usurps Divine prerogatives. Verse 4.
Fourth—He is a blasphemer. Verses 1, 5 and 6.
Fifth—He has superhuman power. Verse 2.
Sixth—He makes war upon the Saints and many fall away. Verses 4, 7 and 15.
Seventh—He comes to his end suddenly. Chapter 19:20, 21.
Eighth—He goes into perdition. Chapters 17:8 and 19:20.
Ninth—He appears in the end time. Chapter 14:7–12.
Tenth—His destruction synchronizes with the coming of the Lord. Chapter 19:11–21.

With these Scriptures before us is it not incontrovertably evident to an unbiased mind that the

"Beast" of Revelation, Paul's "Man of Sin," and Daniel's "Little Horn" are one and the same? and none other than the Anti-Christ? Isaiah prophesied of him before Daniel's day (See Isa. 14:12–17), and the Saviour warns his church against him. (See Matt. 24:23–28.)

The non-prophetic views of the Higher Critics, make it impossible that they should be right eschatologically. And this explains why Antiochus Epiphanes is driven like a coach and four through the prophecies of Daniel. The following very wise and truthful words were written by the late Prof. Delitzsch: "No interpretation of prophecy, on sound principles, is any longer possible from the standpoint of Antichiliasm, inasmuch as the Antichiliasts twist words in the mouths of the prophets and, by their perversion of Scripture, shake the very foundation of all doctrines, everyone of which rests on the plain and simple interpretation of the words of Revelation."

In the eighth chapter, Daniel has another vision which develops the parts of his former vision touched upon most lightly, *i. e.*, the Persian and Grecian Empires. He says nothing concerning Babylon or Rome, and is silent on the subject of the coming of Christ and the Everlasting Kingdom.

In the ninth chapter is a most definite and explicit Messianic prophecy. Verses 24–27. The times of Messiah are here exactly stated. It was seventy Heptades, or periods of seven, *i. e.*, 490 years, from the decree of Cyrus "To restore and to build Jerusalem, unto the Messiah." From 455 B. C., the time Cyrus issued his decree, to A. D. 33. When Christ was "cut off," is 488 years. But, as Christ was born from four to five years before the Christian era, as commonly reckoned, only sixty-nine Heptades have been fulfilled. Therefore Daniel's seventieth week is, without doubt, apocalyptic.

In the ninth and tenth chapters are some prophecies, in detail, that cover the historical period from Cyrus to the domination of the Roman Empire, all of which have been fulfilled.

The twelfth chapter has to do with the end times. The first four verses are as follows:

> And at that time shall Michael stand up, the great prince which standeth for the children of thy people; and there shall be a time of trouble, such as never was since there was a nation even to that same time; and at that time thy people shall be delivered every one that shall be found written in the book. And many of them that sleep in the dust of the earth shall awake, some to everlasting life, and some to shame and everlasting contempt. And they that be wise shall shine as the brightness of the firmament; and they that turn many to righteousness as the stars for ever and ever. But thou, O Daniel, shut up the words, and seal the book, even to the time of the end; many shall run to and fro, and knowledge shall be increased.

Michael is without doubt the angel mentioned in Rev. 20:1, and "That time," is the end of this dispensation. It is the time of "The great tribulation." See Matt. 24:29–31; Rev. 3:5; 13:8; 20:

15. These explain the last clause of the first verse. The second verse has reference to the resurrections, "both of the just and the unjust," which, of course, take place in the end times. Dr. Tregelles renders the verse thus: "Many from among the sleepers of the dust of the earth shall awake, these—that awake —shall be unto everlasting life, and these—the rest of the sleepers—unto shame and everlasting contempt." The Critics do utmost violence to even their own "Literary tests" in spiritualizing such explicit language as Dan. 12:2. Dean Alford, in speaking of such mistreatment of this and similar Scriptural passages, says: "To spiritualize such statements, is to make an end of all significance to language, and wipe out the Bible as a definite testimony to anything."

> Then I Daniel looked and behold, there stood other two, the one on the brink of the river on this side, and the other on the brink of the river on that side. And one said to the man clothed in linen, which was above the waters of the river, How long shall it be to the end of these wonders? And I heard the man clothed in linen, which was above the waters of the river, when he held up his right hand and his left hand unto heaven, and sware by him that liveth for ever that it shall be for a time, times, and an half; and when they have made an end of breaking in pieces the power of the holy people, all these things shall be finished.

Rev. 10:5-8, and, 11:15, 17, 18, will explain the above verses.

The critics will continue their destructive work to the very great delight of infidel scoffers, and thus minister unto their own intellectual pride; but it remains true, incontrovertibly true, that many of the prophecies of Daniel have been fulfilled ; and, by parity of reasoning, we conclude in spite of Higher Critics, and Lower Critics, and enemies of God, and demons, and the power of the "Lawless One," which is already felt, that those that reach onward to the end time will be also, because "No prophecy ever came by the will of man; but men spake from God, being moved by the Holy Ghost." 2 Peter 1 : 21.

"And I heard, but I understood not: then said I, O my lord, what shall be the issue of these things? And he said, Go thy way, Daniel: for the words are shut up and sealed till the time of the end. Many shall purify themselves, and make themselves white, and be refined; but the wicked shall do wickedly; and none of the wicked shall understand: but they that be wise shall understand. And from the time that the continual *burnt offering* shall be taken away, and the abomination that maketh desolate set up, there shall be a thousand two hundred and ninety days. Blessed is he that waiteth, and cometh to the thousand three hundred and five and thirty days. But go thou thy way till the end be; for thou shalt rest, and shalt stand in thy lot, at the end of the days."

CHAPTER XV.

ESTHER.

This Book has been under more or less suspicion from very early times. Dean Stanley says: "Of all the Canonical Books of the Old Testament it is the one which lingered longest on the outskirts, and has provoked the most uneasy suspicion since." This was said with reference to the views entertained of it by the Church of God. The chief cause of such suspicion is the fact that the Septuagint version, while agreeing in the main with the Hebrew text, makes extended and numerous additions thereto. This is doubtless the reason why some of the Church fathers were skeptical as to its genuineness. Melito and Athanasius left it out of their lists of Canonical Books, though its intense Hebrewism may have influenced them somewhat.

It was among the latest books admitted to the Canon, and was placed among the *Hagiographa*. It became, to the Jews, the most precious of them all and was emphatically the roll, "*the Megillah.*" It was believed that it would outlast all the Hebrew Scriptures save the Pentateuch, and that when Messiah would come all the other Scriptures would be done away with save these two.

The Higher Critics insist that the narrative as a whole, seems to read as a romance rather than a history. One says: "It is safer to regard it as historical fiction rather than as veritable history." He goes further and says: "It seems like blasphemy to intimate that God had anything to do with its composition." These views are entertained chiefly because the plot, plan and movement of the narrative are so very dramatic as to seem unhistorical, and the ignoring of the supernatural in their postulates. Canon Driver admits that "Fact, however, is proverbially sometimes stranger than fiction, so that it is somewhat precarious to build a far-reaching argument upon appearances of this nature." The proofs of the historicity of the Book, however, are numerous and convincing. *First*—The verifications by profane history, include the times, customs, events, country and persons mentioned. See Josephus Ant. Book 11, chap. 6, and the Greek histories. Dean Stanley in speaking of the historical situation of the Book, says: "Then come the various scenes of the catastrophy, everyone of which is full of the local genius of the Empire, as we know it, alike through the accounts of the earliest Grecian travelers and the latest English investigators." Canon Driver confesses that "The character of Xerxes, as drawn by him (the writer of Esther) is in agreement with history." The Archæologists have discovered the ruins of Ahasuerus' palace in Shushan, and "In the court of the garden" they found "a pavement of red, and white, and yellow, and black marble," exactly as mentioned in Esther 1:5, 6. *Second*— The Persian words and those of Chaldaic affinity found in the Book, are not found in the older Hebrew texts, and therefore fit the writing to its historic situation. *Third*—The feast of Purim. This feast is held by the Jews to be second in importance to the Feast of the Passover. This latter Feast is observed in commemoration of the passing over of the Death Angel, and sparing the "First Born" of the obedient Israelites, that awful night, when the "First Born" in each Egyptian household was slain. Is it possible that such a Feast as Purim could have been instituted without an historical occasion? Does not the deliverance of God's ancient people, scattered throughout the broad Empire of Persia, as recorded in Esther, exactly suit the case? In Esther 9: 15–28 we have a record of the appointing of the Feast, and we know that it has been observed from that time until now.

A great majority of the ablest exegetes favor the historic view, among them such distinguished scholars as Baumgarten, Havernick, Keil, Staehelin, Berthen and Ewald.

AUTHORSHIP.

Eichhorn, Keil and others put this writing in the reign of Artaxerxes 464—425 B. C. Rawlinson fixes it 444—434 B. C. It has always been recorded in the Jewish canon. Humanly speaking no one could write the Book personally unfamiliar with the laws and customs of the Persian court. The details of the narrative justify such a view of the case. There is no one of whom we have any knowledge who could possibly do this work save "Mordecai the Jew." We find in him all the prerequisites for such a work. In chapters 8 : 8–10, and 9 : 20, 23, 29 it is recorded that he did some writing, and was, therefore, somewhat of a scribe. Beside, he was personally familiar with all the facts in the case. However, in the absence of any explicit testimony of the Highest Critics as to the authorship of this Book, we may not insist on our view; but, after carefully weighing all the evidence pro. and con., we express it as our conviction that " Mordecai the Jew" wrote the Book of Esther.

It is urged by the Critics that the ferocious and blood-thirsty spirit manifested by Esther and Mordecai was not Christ-like, and, therefore, the Book is not inspired, and should never have been admitted into the Jewish canon. Exodus, Numbers, Deuteronomy, Joshua, Judges, the Books of the Chronicles, and The Psalms, by the same ruling, ought not to have been admitted to the canon ; for Moses, Joshua, Gideon and David were men of blood and slaughter. But the ferocity and blood-thirstiness of Esther and Mordecai is greatly magnified by the Critics. Let the whole situation be taken into the account, as well as the times and people, and dispassionately considered, and I am sure their criticism is not justified. Let it also be remembered that they were living under law and not under grace, and then it will be understood why so few comparatively of the Old Testament heroes were in any sense Christ-like.

The Critics deny the inspiration of the Book because the name of God does not once occur in it. Ewald says: "In passing from other Books of the

Old Testament to Esther, we fall from heaven to earth." Canon Driver says: "It is remarkable that whereas generally in the Old Testament, national and religious interests are commingled, they are here divorced: the national being extremely strong, and the religious feeling being practically absent altogether." The Critic finds what he wants to find. How any one can be spiritually minded and prayerfully study the Book of Esther, and write such a statement as the above, is more than I can understand. Dean Stanley saw it otherwise for he says: "The name of God is *not there*, but the work of God *is*."

When it is remembered that the Jews but seldom wrote or spoke the name of God, and when they did it was with a profound and awe inspiring reverence, it is not at all surprising that it is not mentioned in this Book, written as it was in the land of the stranger.

But let us examine it a little closely and see if we can find any Spiritual lessons. Dr. Pierson says, "The doctrine of God's Providence finds here a historical and pictorial parable." *First*—There is behind human affairs an unseen hand guiding and directing according to the purposes of God in mercy and grace. (Isa. 58:11; Psa. 25:9.) Wherever in God's Word was this fact more clearly and forcibly set forth? *Second*—Both evil and good have their ultimate awards. (Jno. 5:28, 29; 2 Cor. 5:10; Rev. 22:18.) *Third*—The prosperity and exhaltation of the wicked is unsatisfying and shortlived and terminates in adversity. (Psa. 92:7; 73:3; 17:20.) *Fourth*—The adversity of the good is a trial of faith, issuing in prosperity. (Heb. 12:5-11; Rom. 8:28.) *Fifth*—Retribution is administered with poetic exactness. (Gal. 6:7; Rev. 20:13.) *Sixth*—The most minute events are woven into God's plan. (Matt. 10:29-31; Acts 27:34.) *Seventh*—Providence is not fate, but consists with prayer and resolve, freedom and responsibility. (James 1:17; Phil. 4:19; 1 John 5:13, 14.)

The doctrine of substitution is beautifully suggested by Esther's willingness to die for the people, a voluntary and vicarious sacrifice. Esther's communication with the King suggests the believer's fellowship with the King of Glory. (See Jno. 14:23, and 1 Jno. 1:7.) Esther's marriage suggests the relations of Christ and His Bride—the Church. (See 2 Cor. 11:2; Eph. 5:22-27; Matt. 25:1-12.) The answers she received to her supplications are quite in line with the doctrine of acceptable prayer. The unlimited and innumerable promises of God are typified in Esther 8:8. The final victory over all her foes, is what is at last to be gloriously true of the Bride of Jesus Christ. (Rev. 21:7; 3:21.)

Let us examine a little closer and we shall find a rich mine of eschatalogical truth: Ahasuerus' was a mighty monarch (See Chap. 1:1-4), and in his regal splendor was a type of Jesus as King, when He shall reign from the rivers unto the ends of the earth. (See Isa. 9:6, 7; Luke 1:31-33; Rev. 11:15-17; Phil. 2:9-11; Rev. 5:11-13.)

Vashti is a type of Israel. She was the lawful wife of Ahasuerus, but was banished and another took her place. Because of Israel's rejection of Messiah she is now in the dispersion, the lawful undivorced wife of God the Father Almighty (Isa. 54: 5 and Jer. 3: 12-14). But she will return from her wanderings, and be restored to Divine favor and honor (Rom. 11: 26; Rev. 7: 4-8). In commenting upon Esther 2: 1, where it is said "When the wrath of King Ahasuerus was appeased, he remembered Vashti," Jehoshaphet Ben Ezra, in his book entitled "The Coming of Messiah in Glory and Majesty," says: "The time shall come when King Ahasuerns shall remember Vhasti and what she hath done, and what was decreed against her. The time shall come in which his heart shall move towards his former spouse, whom he put away from him for righteous reasons; when taking pity upon her hardships and softened by her tears; and satisfied with her great and most sorrowful repentance, he shall call her once more to himself, and shall reinstate her in all her honors, and clothe her with greater glory than she was possessed of before her misfortunes."

Esther is a type of the Church. In this dispensation of the Spirit, God is taking from among the nations a people that were no people (See Hosea 2: 23, and Rom. 9: 25, 26), as a bride for His Son (See Hosea 2: 19, 20, and 2 Cor. 11: 2). And so the rejection of Israel has turned out to our account who are called from among the Gentiles (See Rom. 11: 11-15).

Haman is a type of the anti-Christ. The anti-Christ is Daniel's "Little Horn" (Dan. 7:8), Paul's "Man of Sin" (2 Thess. 2:3), and John's "Beast" with the wounded head (Rev. 13:3). He is a usurper, and like Haman, will come to his end suddenly. (See Dan 7:11.; Phil. 2:8, and Rev. 19:20, 21.)

Haman's ten sons are types of the "ten kings" mentioned in Dan. 7:24, and Rev. 17:12–18.

The "Great feast" King Ahasuerus made for Esther, chapter 2:9, 17, 18, most beautifully typifies the "Marriage Supper of the Lamb." (See Matt. 25:1–12, and Rev. 19:7, 8, 17.)

King Ahasuerus shared equally his honors and possessions with Esther. See chapter 5:3. This is just what the King of Kings will do with His Bride —the Church, in His coming kingdom and glory. See Luke 22:29, 30, and Rev. 3:21. And so, in falling "from heaven to earth," as Ewald puts it, it is plain to be seen by one who has spiritual vision, that we bring much of heaven with us, for there is much of that which is heavenly in the Book of Esther, to be seen by the heavenly minded.

The Highest Critics bear no direct testimony to the authorship and authenticity of this Book. But since it belongs to the Writings which the Holy Spirit says were "Given by inspiration of God," we know that it was God-given; "For no prophecy ever came by the will of men; but men spake from God, being moved by the Holy Ghost." May God smite with the might of his power the destructive criticisms of the Higher Critics. Amen!

CHAPTER XVI.

WORK OF THE CRITICS COMPARED.

We hear a great deal in these days about "Modern Biblical Study," "Wonderful Progress," "Advanced Thought," "Marvelous Discoveries," etc., etc., as applied to biblical study and knowledge. These expressions, oft repeated as they are, impress the young and ignorant with the twofold idea that we have mastered well-nigh all the difficulties belonging to such study, and that preceding generations knew little or nothing, critically and scientifically, of the Word of God.

Some of the theories and methods of some of the Higher Critics are indeed "wonderful" and "marvelous," and quite altogether "modern," and may also be characterized as ingenious, unique, and startling, and also very presumptuous and exceedingly audacious.

Advancement *has* been made along right lines, for which all lovers of God's Word are truly thankful.

But what is said about Moses not being the writer of the Pentateuch, about these writings being largely made up of myths, legends, traditions, fables, and sagas borrowed from the surrounding nations; and about their historic, chronologic, and scientific inaccuracies and unreliability is only "threshing old straw."

Many of the criticisms, if not all, were made by Aben Ezra in 1168, by Carlstadt in 1541, by Andreas Maes in 1573, by Hobbs in 1651, by Spinoza in 1670, by Jean Astruc in 1753, and by Eichhorn in 1779.

There is not a single objection raised by modern Higher Criticism against the integrity of the Old Testament Scriptures that was not urged by Voltaire one hundred and thirty years ago, and may be found in the sixth volume of the Didot edition of his works. The same may be said of Paine's Age of Reason, believed by many to be the most damaging book to Christianity ever written.

More than one hundred years ago certain learned Jewish rabbis, who knew their language, traditions, and Book far better than most modern Higher Critics, wrote quite a number of letters to Voltaire, in which all his objections were most satisfactorily met and his questions convincingly answered. These letters are in book form, and bear the title The Jew's Letters to Voltaire. So completely and overwhelmingly did these rabbis route Voltaire that we need nothing more with which to meet the objections raised against the integrity of the Old Testament Scriptures by the modern critic.

I wish to quote from three classes of critics, viz.: Infidel, Rationalist, and Supernaturalist, as to the authorship, character, and reliability of the Pentateuch, that the reader may see how nearly they agree in these matters.

The infidels are Voltaire, Paine, and Ingersoll. The rationalists are Kuenen, Wellhausen, Dillmann, Cornill, Robertson Smith, Prof. Cheyne, B. W. Bacon, and Prof. Ladd.* The supernaturalists are Riehm, Schultz, Driver, Briggs, and Harper.

The infidels are, of course, bitterly antagonistic to the Bible and Christianity.

The rationalists deny a supernatural element in the Bible, reducing it to the level of other so-called sacred writings at the last analysis, thus making it a merely human production, and yet claim to believe in Christianity.

The supernaturalists claim—some of them—that the Bible is God's Word. Some of them insist that it contains God's Word. They all believe that parts of the Bible are somehow inspired of God, but they seem not to know how, and are not at all agreed as to what parts. They all profess to be Orthodox Christians, and are so recognized in their denominations.

First, then, as to the *Authorship of the Pentateuch.*

Voltaire said: "It is said, even in their books, that this Pentateuch was not known until the reign of their king, Josiah, thirty-six years before the destruction and captivity of Jerusalem, and then they only possessed a single copy which the priest, Hil-

---

* Classifying Profs. Smith, Cheyne, and Ladd and Dr. Bacon among rationalists, is only stating my opinion of the views of these gentlemen, after reading carefully their writings on biblical criticism.

kiah, found at the bottom of a strong box while counting money." "The book found under Josiah was unknown until the return from the Babylonian captivity." (Phil. Dictionary, Art. "Moses," 1762.)

"Almost all men well acquainted with antiquity agree that this book (the Pentateuch) was not issued among the Jews until the time of Ezra. * * * The greatest proof to some learned men that Ezra edited all the Jewish books is that they appear to be in the same style." (God and Men, 1769, Chap. 19.)

"Those best acquainted with antiquity think that these books were written more than seven hundred years after Moses." (Dialogue 16.)

"It has been supposed that the whole Pentateuch was written by some Levites eight hundred and twenty-seven years after Moses (according to the Vulgate), in the time of Josiah." (Bible Explained, 1777, "Deut.")

"Toland assures us that it is plain that all these books were written a long time after (the events) by some lazy priest, * * * and that we ought not to believe the Pentateuch any more than the Sibylline books which were regarded sacred during centuries." (Bible Explained, 1777, Exodus, Chap. 19.)

"I am asked who is the author of the Pentateuch? One may as well ask me who wrote the Four Sons of Aymon, Robert the Devil, or the History of the Enchanter, Merlin." (Important Examination, 1767, Chap. 4.)

"The Pentateuch could not be from Moses." (Ex. of Lord Bolingbroke.)

Paine said: "All the contradictions in time, place, and circumstances that abound in the books ascribed to Moses prove to a demonstration that those books could not be written by Moses, nor in the time of Moses." (P. 89.) * "The style and manner in which those books are written give no room to believe, or even to suppose, that they were written by Moses." (P. 80.) "From the historical and chronological evidence contained in these books, Moses was not, because he could not be, the writer of them." (P. 82.) "My intention is to show that those books are spurious, and that Moses is not the author of them; and still further, that they were not written in the time of Moses, nor till several hundred years afterwards." (P. 80.) "It cannot be admitted as a fact in those books that it is Moses who speaks, without rendering Moses truly ridiculous and absurd." (P. 80.) "Moses is not the author of the books ascribed to him." (P. 87.) "The Book of Genesis, though it is placed first in the Bible and ascribed to Moses, has been manufactured by some unknown person, after the Book of Chronicles was written, which was not until at least eight hundred and sixty years after the time of Moses." (P. 99.) "Though it is impossible for us to know *identically* who the writer of Deuteronomy was, it is

---

* The quotations from Paine are all taken from The Theological Works of Thomas Paine, Boston, J. P. Mendum, 1854.

not difficult to discover him professionally, that he was some Jewish priest who lived, as I shall show in the course of this work, at least three hundred and fifty years after the time of Moses." (P. 83.) "In Deuteronomy the style and manner of writing marks more evidently than the former books that Moses is not the writer." (P. 81.) "If Moses was not the author (of Numbers), the books are without authority." (P. 81.) "Those who have superstitiously boasted of the antiquity of the Bible, and particularly the books ascribed to Moses, have done it without examination and without any authority than that of one credulous man telling it to another; for, so far as historical and chronological evidence applies, the very first book in the Bible is not so ancient as the book of Homer by more than three hundred years, and is about the same age with Æsop's Fables." (P. 92.)

Ingersoll says in his last lecture About the Holy Bible, New York, C. P. Farrell, 1894: "Many centuries after Moses, the leader, was dead—many centuries after all his followers had passed away—the Pentateuch was written, the work of many writers, and to give it force and authority it was claimed that Moses was its author. We now know that the Pentateuch was not written by Moses." (P. 8.) "It is now not only admitted by intelligent and honest theologians that Moses was not the author of the Pentateuch, but they all admit that no one knows who the authors were, or who wrote any of these books, or a chapter, or a line. We know that the books were not written in the same generation; that they were not written by any one person." (P. 9.)

Kuenen says: "Utterly unhistorical, and therefore cannot have been committed to writing until centuries after Moses and Joshua." (The Hexateuch, Wicksteed's translation, p. 42.) "The representations of the Hexateuch, as they stand, can only be regarded as the products of ages long after Moses and Joshua." (P. 48.) "Most of them (the elements of the Hexateuch) are remote from the age of Moses and Joshua." (P. 48.)

Wellhausen says: "Somewhat later (B. C. 850–750), perhaps the legends about the patriarchs and primitive times, the origin of which cannot be assigned to a very early date." "Even the Jehovistic narratives about the patriarchs belong to the time when Israel had already become a powerful kingdom." (Hist. of Israel and Judah, p. 71.)

Dillmann says: "The style of Deuteronomy implies a long development of the art of public oratory, and is not of a character to belong to the first age of Israelitish literature." (P. 611.) He held that *P.* was written B. C. 900, in the kingdom of Judah; and that *E.* was written in the Northern Kingdom in the first half of the ninth century before Christ; while *J.* was written in the Southern Kingdom not earlier than the middle of eighth century B. C.

Cornill says: "The old historical books and the

Pentateuch exclude each the other. Either the representation of the historical books is true, and then the Pentateuch cannot be the foundation of Mosaism and of the religion of Israel; or, the Pentateuchal laws are from Moses, and then the representation of the historical books cannot be true." (Intro. to O. T., p. 272.)

Cheyne says: "Deuteronomy was composed * * * by no possibility later than the eighteenth year of the reign of Josiah. * * * Hilkiah may possibly have had to do with the composition of the book." (Founders of O. T. Crit., pp. 271-272.)

Robertson Smith says: "The Pentateuch, then, is a history incorporating at least three bodies of laws. The history does not profess to be written by Moses." (The Old Testament in the Jewish Church, p. 323.) "As a matter of fact, the Pentateuchal history was written in the land of Canaan, and if it is all by one hand it was not composed before the period of the Kings." (P. 325.) "The Pentateuch in its present form was written after the time of Moses, nay, after that of Joshua. We cannot venture to assert that the composition of the Pentateuch out of older sources of various date took place before the time of the Kings." (P. 331.) "The narrative in its present form cannot be older than the youngest body of laws, and therefore must have been completed some time between the age of Ezekiel and that of Ezra." (P. 388.) "No part of Deuteronomy 1-30 can be older than the seventh century B. C., while * * * some parts may be a good deal later than Josiah's Reformation in B. C. 621." (P. 394.) "But the mass of the Hexateuch, after Deuteronomy 1-30 has been set on one side, is made up of extracts from several sources pieced together in a complicated way." (P. 396.) "The priestly document or group * * * after Ezekiel, as the historic-legal argument requires." (P. 408.)

Prof. Ladd says: "Undoubtedly the first six books of the Bible are a composite literary structure, the sources and materials of which came from different times and authors; *they could not, therefore, have been all the work of Moses.*" (What is the Bible? p. 312.) "The venerable tradition, more than two thousand years old, which asserts the Mosaic authorship of the entire Pentateuch, stands opposed to the almost unanimous verdict of modern biblical study. The tradition, although it is so ancient, has absolutely no valid claims that justify its uncritical acceptance." (P. 302.) "The whole world of scholars has abandoned the ancient tradition that the Pentateuch, in any such form as we now have it, was the work of Moses." (P. 300.)

Dr. B. W. Bacon says: "There are practically none to hold to the main contention of the traditionalists, an origin within the Mosaic age for any considerable part of the narrative material." (The Hexateuch, New York Independent, May 3, 1894.)

Schultz says: "For the latest writers of the Pentateuch it was an accepted fact that all the religious knowledge and all the sacred institutions of Israel that were in actual existence down to the time of Ezra had been received from God by Moses. * * * This view is not that of Israel's early reminiscences, and no historical inquirer of the present day will advocate it." (O. T. Theo., p. 132.)

Dr. Driver says: "Even though it were clear that the first four books of the Pentateuch were written by Moses, it would be difficult to sustain the Mosaic authorship of Deuteronomy." (Introduction to the Lit. of the Old Testament, p. 77.) "The Mosaic authorship of Genesis to Numbers cannot be sustained." * * * "The historical books afford a strong presumption that the law of Deuteronomy did not originate until after the establishment of the monarchy." (P. 80.) "Deuteronomy does not claim to be written by Moses." (P. 83.) "Neither (*J.* and *E.*) is later than about B. C. 750." (P. 116.) "They resemble the best parts of Judges and Samuel (much of which cannot be greatly later than David's own time). And there are certain passages in which language is used implying that the period of the Exodus is in the past, and that Israel is established in Canaan." (P. 117.) "It (the *P.* document) is itself the latest of the sources of which the Hexateuch is composed, and belongs approximately to the period of the Babylonian captivity." (P. 129.) "The *completed* Priest's Code is the work of the age subsequent to Ezekiel." (P. 135.)

Prof. Briggs says: "Moses did not write the Pentateuch." (Defense of Prof. Briggs. New York: Charles Scribner's Sons, pp. 120, 127, 128.) "It may be regarded as the certain result of the science of the Higher Criticism that Moses did not write the Pentateuch." (Inaugural, p. 33.)

Pres. Harper says: "The present literary form of this revelation, Gen. 1-11, dates from about that period," B. C. 900. (Biblical World, vol. 4, p. 415.) "Should criticism prove that the larger portion of the Mosaic system, as we have it to-day, arose in a post-Mosaic period, it would not in any way contradict the representations made in the New Testament." (P.414.) "At a later period—how much later is and always will be a matter of uncertainty—an editor * * * undertakes to join these various representations—Gen. 1-11—together." (P. 412.)

Second. The Character of the Pentateuch.

Voltaire said: "Is it not plain that Genesis was taken from the ancient fables of their (the Jews') neighbors?" "The Fable of Moses," "The Fable of the Pentateuch." (Ex. of Lord Bolingbroke.)

Paine said: "Take away from Genesis the belief that Moses was its author, on which only the strange belief that it is the Word of God has stood, and there remains nothing in Genesis but an anonymous book of stories, fables, and traditionary or invented absurdities, or of downright lies." (Age of Reason, p. 86.)

Ingersoll says: "We also know that the account of the Tower of Babel is an ignorant and childish fable." (P. 24.)

Kuenen says: "We can no longer accept his statements as true (the Flood). We cannot give any high position to the legend itself." (The Bible for Learners, p. 76.) "Legend plays a greater part than history itself in the accounts we possess of him" (Moses). (P. 242.) "The sagas about the patriarchs, the exodus, and the conquest." (P. 226.)

Wellhausen says: "It dresses itself up in archaistic fashion." (History of Israel, p. 41.) "The historical tradition which has reached us relating to the period of the judges and of the kings of Israel is the main source, though only of course in an indirect way, of our knowledge of Mosaism." (P. 18.) "The Jews had no historical life, and therefore painted the old time according to their ideas, and framed the time to come according to their wishes." (P. 213.)

Dillmann says: "When he (the Redactor of the Hexateuch) had no historical accounts he sketches freely an imaginary picture." (Numb., Josh., and Deut., p. 650.) "The oral saga within which falls all the history given by *P*. He knew and used the North Israelite book of sagas." (P. 655.)

Prof. Cheyne says: "And neither by him (Prof. Sayce), nor by anyone else, has it yet been made probable that there was a historical individual among the ancestors of the Israelites called Abram,* or that the picture of the times of Abraham in Genesis is (to adopt Prof. Ramsay's phrase) a fundamentally true tale, except, indeed, so far as it reflects the times of the narrators." (Founders of O. T. Criticism, p. 239.)

Robertson Smith says: " He (*P.*) chooses a canvas as large as that of the pre-priestly Torah, and throws the exposition of the system of Israel's sacred ordinances into the form of history from the Creation to the complete settlement in Canaan. This whole history his plan compels him to idealize or allegorize, and he does so boldly." (O. T. in Jewish Church.)

Prof. Ladd says: "The traditions of the first chapter of Genesis." (What is the Bible? p. 71.) "The knowledge of these facts, too, can be shown to have come to the author of Genesis solely in the ordinary way of tradition or of written documents." (P. 194.) " The picture of the Garden of Eden, or place where life began, is also a traditional one."

---

* Prof. Meinhold, at the last Bonn Vacation course of lectures, claimed that the biblical accounts of the patriarchs Abraham, Isaac, and Jacob are entirely unhistorical, and that the whole patriarchal history of Israel is a myth, and that this view is the necessary conclusion of the documentary theory of the Pentateuch. The theological faculty at Bonn addressed a circular letter to the eight other Protestant faculties in Prussia asking if these opinions were contrary to the confessional status of the Church. With the sole exception of Griefswald the faculties answered that such views were permissible within the evangelical Church, and that to maintain them was not in conflict with the confessional.

Of course, if Abraham is a myth, Jesus Christ is a myth also, for he is the " Son of Abraham," and the "Covenant of Grace" stands for nothing, and we are without hope, "and of all men most miserable." Being but myths ourselves, for believers " are the children of Abraham " (Gal. 3. 7), it is a matter of no special importance. Can anything be more destructive? The infidels never said anything worse against the truth of the Bible—never!

(P. 197.) "The remarkable similarity of some of these traditions (Creation, the Fall, the Flood) to the early chapters of Genesis has suggested a common origin for both." (P. 68.)

Schultz says: "We can do nothing more than draw inferences from the national legends we have, and from fragments of myth and of ancient customs that remain." (O. T. Theo., p. 73.)

Riehm says: "In the earliest history we find ourselves on the ground of sacred saga. Either this history must have been given to the narrators by revelation or by historical archives in addition to the popular saga. Neither is the fact. Thus it is *a priori* probable that these narratives were taken from the popular saga. Their peculiar character makes on the unprejudiced mind the clear impression that they are not history, but saga." (Int. to O. T., p. 340.)

Prof. Driver says: "None of the historians of the Bible claim supernatural enlightenment for the *materials* of their narrative. It is reasonable, therefore, to conclude that these were derived by them from such human sources as were at the disposal of each particular writer—in some cases from a writer's own personal knowledge, in others from earlier documentary sources; in others, especially in those relating to a distant past, from popular tradition." (Int. to Lit. O. T., Preface XII.)

. Pres. Harper says: "These stories" (Bible Accounts of the Origin of Man) "are not history, for the times are prehistoric times. They are the Hebrew version (purged and purified) of the best thoughts of humanity in that earliest period when man stood alone with nature and with God. It is sacrilege to call them history. They are *stories*. * * * Let us be careful not to credit to the Holy Spirit, who kindled the fire of inspiration, the ignorance and superstition of those in whose hearts the fire was not kindled." (Biblical World, vol. 3, p. 108.) "He takes the stories" (Bible Account of Paradise and the First Sin) "common to all ancient nations. * * * He does what the prophet always does—he idealizes." (P. 188.) "It seems probable that the biblical story of the sons of God and the daughters of men has a common origin with outside stories. * * * The story is something our writer finds at hand. As he finds it, it is a legend. He purifies it." (P. 188.) "Some of its illustrations—Heb., chapter xi—could be shown to be drawn from religious stories commonly accepted as historical narratives, but in reality generically or ideally true, rather than in the modern sense of the term historically." (Vol. 3, p. 164.)

Third. Reliability.

Voltaire said: "Their chronology is always erroneous." "The innumerable mistakes of geography, of chronology, and the contradictions found in the Pentateuch." (Ex. of Lord Bolingbroke.)

Paine said: "I am not undertaking to point out all the contradictions in time, place, and circumstances that abound in the books ascribed to Moses." (P. 89, A. of R.)

Ingersoll says: "Genesis contradicts itself. There are two accounts of the Flood." (About the Holy Bible, p. 23.) "We know that the story of the Flood is much older than the book of Genesis, and we know, besides, that it is not true." (P. 24.) "A dreary and detailed statement (Genesis) of things that never happened." (P. 25.)

Kuenen says: "As a rule they concern themselves very little with the question whether what they narrate really happened so or not. This is why the Old and New Testament are so full of legends." (Bible for Learners, p. 5.) In his Hexateuch he says: "It is in *P.* that the absolutely unhistorical representation of Israel's settlement in the trans-Jordanic district and of the division of Canaan by lot is most fully developed."

"He (*P.*) shows little care for the reality, and subordinates historical probability to considerations of quite another order." (P. 173.) "The representation of the Mosaic times and of the settlement in Canaan which the Hexateuch gives us is, as a whole, contradicted by the veritable history." (P. 192.) "The exodus, the wandering, the passage of the Jordan, and the settlement in Canaan, as they are described in the Hexateuch are simply impossible." (P. 43.) "The representation of all this (the exodus) in the Hexateuch is absurd." (P. 46.)

Wellhausen says: "The historical sphere created out of its own premises is nowhere to be found in actual history." (P. 41, Hist. of Israel.) "It is full of historical fiction." (P. 170.) "All confidence in it is lost." (P. 334.) "Its incredible insipidity; it is hard to give an idea of its pedantry." (P. 331.) "Indescribable pedantry of language accompanies the intellectual pedantry." (P. 336.) Thus this Higher Critic speaks of the first four chapters of Genesis.

Dillmann says: "Noah's ark, course of the Flood, tabernacle (after the manner of a movable holy tent, richly furnished), the order of the camp and march (in geometrical divisions), the determination of the boundaries of the tribes by lot under Joshua, the members of each tribe in Moses' day, the quantity of manna that fell, etc. They are not to be taken historically." (Numb., Josh., and Deut., p. 650.)

Cornill, in his Introduction to Old Testament, says (p. 56): "*P.* contains contradictions and inconceivable things." (P. 272.) "All historical value must be denied to him." "A narrator whose untrustworthiness is proved." (P. 63.) "The tabernacle * * * is merely a carrying back of the Deuteronomic central sanctuary; that is, the temple of Solomon into the time of Moses, after it had been made movable through a waste of wit not to be despised."

Robertson Smith says: "The conclusion to which modern critics have been led is that the whole Priest's Code, alike in those parts which are formally legislative and in those which a superficial reading might regard as purely historical, is to be taken as essentially a law-book, and must not be used as an independent source for the actual history of the Mosaic times." (O. T. in Jewish Church, p. 387.)

Prof. Cheyne says: "The historical fact of the Hittite conquest has come down to the writer symbolized as *P.* in a meager and scarcely recognizable form, and has become the setting of a tradition of uncertain date." (Founders of O. T. Criticism, p. 240.)

Prof. Ladd says: "The same primitive and unscientific character belongs to those classifications of the animals and descriptions of natural phenomena which are found in the Mosaic cosmogony, in the narrative of the Deluge and in the Mosaic law." (P. 134, What is the Bible?) "The biblical writers show no signs of having been inspired so as to be errorless when treating of physical matters; they make the mistakes incident to their times." "There is not an atom of evidence to show that they had any other information concerning the truths of nature than such as belonged to all their contemporaries." (P. 135.) "Nowhere else in the entire Bible do we find narratives the genuine historical character of which is more doubtful, and the moral and religious value obvious, than those of the fourth, fifth, and early part of the sixth chapters of Genesis." (P. 198.)

Dr. Bacon says: " Many, doubtless will continue to cling to the tradition of the Mosaic authorship of the Pentateuch, as men long clung to the Davidic authorship of the Psalms. But those who have witnessed the quiet superseding of this now obsolete idea by that of historical criticism, presenting the Psalmbook as a conglomerate which unites in one collection fruits of the religious thought and feeling of Israel during many centuries, have no excuse for regarding the exactly analogous treatment of the heterogeneous elements of the Hexateuch as necessarily subversive of religious faith." (Gen. of Gen., p. 64.)

Riehm says: " Not only did they (the authors of the Pentateuch) compose the speeches of the actors, as freely as Thucydides or Livy, but they also gave themselves to more or less free reconstruction of the popular tradition."   (Intro. to O. T., vol. 1, p. 339.)

Schultz says: " The work of a priest who, undeterred by the existence of sanctuaries in Israel, has presented us with his ideal of sacred customs in the form of a history."   (O. T. Theo., p. 73.)

Driver says: " It is difficult to escape the conclusion that the representation of *P.* includes elements not, in the ordinary sense of the term, historical." (Intro. O. T., p. 120.) " It is probable that, being a priest himself, he recorded traditions, at least to a certain extent, in the form in which they were current in priestly circles." (P. 121.) " The partition of the land being conceived as ideally effected by

Joshua, its complete distribution and occupation by the tribes are treated as his work, and as accomplished in his lifetime." (P. 108.)

Prof. Briggs says : " These human features render it improbable that the Bible should be free from errors in its human setting. The psychology may be crude, the methods of reasoning sometimes inexact, the rhetoric occasionally extravagant, the language of some of the writers rude, their conceptions provincial, their knowledge of the earth defective. But how could it be otherwise if the divine revelation was to come through such men as the ancient times were capable of producing? Holy Scripture does not claim inerrancy in its human setting, and it does not in fact possess it." (The Bible, the Church, and the Reason, p. 108.) "I have maintained that there are errors in the texts which we have and in the best texts which we can get by the science of textual criticism, and that it is improbable that the original texts, if we could discover them, would be much different from those we have in that regard. "(The Defense of Prof. Briggs Before the Presb. of New York, p. 105.) "I shall venture to affirm that, so far as I can see, there are errors in the Scriptures that no one has been able to explain away; and the theory that they were not in the original text is sheer assumption. * * * If such errors destroy the authority of the Bible, it is already destroyed for historians." (Inaugural, p. 35.)

Pres. Harper says: "The fact universally accepted that in the present manuscripts and versions of our Bible there are errors and inaccuracies." (Biblical World, vol. 4, p. 415.) "One may well doubt whether it was really the purpose of the writer to express the thought which has been commonly taken from his words." (Concerning the Flood, p. 29.)

"It is not historical, in the proper sense of the word. The names are ideal names gathered from the stories known to all the world. The number of names, ten, is ideal. The number of years each patriarch lived is not known." (Vol. 3, p. 334.) "Do we expect of the early times a perfect morality? or a morality judged by the standard of our times? Then why expect a perfect historiography?" (Vol. 4, p. 199.) "Why then should we look for the highest form of literary composition? We know that it was a child age." (P. 200.) "Is it literal history? (the Deluge). No. Nor is the Book of Job history, nor the Books of Chronicles, nor the Books of Kings, nor the Books of Samuel." (P. 120.)

"It has been seen that the representations made concerning the Garden of Eden, its situation and its rivers, are ideal representations; that at no period in the history of investigation has it been possible to determine the details; that the elements in the representation are found in the same forms in other ancient accounts; that these do not accord strictly with geographical science. It has been seen that the great ages assigned to the patriarchs are not borne out by history and are contrary to the teachings of physiological science; that a table of nations is given which purports to be ethnological and to include all the descendants of Noah, in which, however, many omissions are to be found— a table which, indeed, omits certain great races altogether, and which, therefore, cannot be called a scientific table. These are a few of many important variations between what seem to be the implications of the narratives and the results of science. * * * If the Holy Spirit undertook to reveal a scientific knowledge of things to men in those days, the revelation made was of a strange and peculiar character. Really it is nothing short of blasphemy to attribute these things to the Holy Spirit." (P. 276.) "If we deny it, we certainly assume a grave responsibility in attributing to the Holy Spirit that which is dishonoring and degrading." (P. 275.)

"If there is an analysis the sacred record can no longer be claimed to present a perfectly accurate account of the early times, for conflicting accounts stand side by side, changes have been arbitrarily introduced into the text, insertions and omissions have been made, the material cannot be called in a strict sense historical.

"If there is an analysis there are two, though perhaps not contradictory, conceptions of God, one of which seems to border closely on polytheism.

How is it possible for so low an idea of God to have been incorporated in the sacred Scriptures?

"If all this is true the character of the Old Testament material, whether viewed (*a*) from an archæological, (*b*) from an historical, and especially (*c*) from a religious point of view, must be estimated somewhat differently from the method commonly in vogue. It is composed of different stories of the same event, joined together by an editor who did not have insight sufficient to enable him to see that he was all the time committing grave blunders, and yet felt no hesitancy in altering the originals with which he was working. It is not historical in the ordinary sense of that word." (Hebraica, Oct., 1888, pp. 68-70.)

We see by these criticisms that with a very few unimportant qualifications, variations, and reservations there is striking agreement between these three classes of critics upon the three points under consideration, viz.: *First*—That Moses was not the author of the Pentateuch, and that it was not written or edited until from four hundred to one thousand years after his death by persons wholly unknown. *Second*—That the Pentateuch, especially Genesis, is made up largely of myths, legends, fables, sagas, and traditions; and, *Third*—That, historically, chronologically, and scientifically, these writings are untrustworthy.

All this means: *First*—If Moses did not write the Pentateuch, its own claims as to authorship are false, the Old Testament prophets did not tell the truth in their testimony upon this subject, and Jesus and the apostles were wholly ignorant of this matter or knowingly condoned a falsehood and perpetuated a fraud.* *Second*—That the Pentateuch is not God's word at all in any real sense ; but, being made up of myths, fables, and legends, borrowed or stolen from the heathen about them, and the traditions of men, is not binding upon the consciences and lives of men. *Third*—A denial of inspiration. If this record is as unreliable as these gentlemen agree it is, it is a sin before high heaven to say it is inspired of God, or that it is God's Word.

Here is what Thomas Paine, Christianity's great enemy, says upon this point:

"Combining, then, all the foregoing circumstances together respecting the antiquity and authenticity of the Book of Genesis, a conclusion will naturally follow therefrom. Those circumstances are : *First*—That certain parts of the book cannot possibly have been written by Moses, and the other parts carry no evidence of having been written by him. *Second*—

---

* Herman L. Strack says: "As regards passages from the New Testament, we must protest against their use for the twofold reason, that if they prove the Mosaic authorship all other proofs are superfluous and are a derogation from the authority of our Lord, and that the use of such proofs removes the whole question from the historical and critical domain." (Schaff-Herzog Encyclopedia.)

Kuenen says: "The exegesis of the writers of the New Testament cannot stand before the tribunal of science. We must either cast aside as worthless our dearly bought scientific method, or must forever cease to acknowledge the authority of the New Testament in the domain of the exegesis of the Old. Without hesitation we choose the latter alternative." (Prophets and Prophecy in Israel, p. 487.)

The universal silence of all the following books of the Bible, for about a thousand years, upon the extraordinary things spoken of in Genesis, such as the creation of the world in six days, the Garden of Eden, the tree of knowledge, the tree of life, the story of Eve and the serpent, the fall of man, and his being turned out of this fine garden, together with Noah's flood and the Tower of Babel. *Third*—The silence of all the books of the Bible upon even the name of Moses, from the Book of Joshua until the second Book of Kings, which was not written until after the captivity, a period of about a thousand years. Strange that a man who is proclaimed as the historian of Creation, the privy counselor and confidant of the Almighty, the legislator of the Jewish nation, and the founder of its religion—strange, I say, that even the name of such a man should not find a place in their books for a thousand years if they knew or believed anything about him, or the books he is said to have written." "*Fourth*—The opinion of some of the most celebrated of the Jewish commentators, that Moses is not the author of the Book of Genesis, founded on the reasons given for that opinion. *Fifth*—The opinion of the early Christian writers and of the great champion of Jewish literature, Maimonides, that the Book of Genesis is not a book of facts. *Sixth*—The silence imposed by all the Jewish rabbis, and by Maimonides himself, upon the Jewish nation, not to speak of anything they happen to know or discover respecting the cosmogony (or creation of the world) in the Book of Genesis.

"From these circumstances the following circumstances offer:

"*First*—That the Book of Genesis is not a book of facts. *Second*—That as no mention is made throughout the Bible of any of the extraordinary things related in Genesis, that it has not been written till after the other books were written, and put as a preface to the Bible. Everyone knows that a preface to a book, though it stands first, is the last written. *Third*—That the silence imposed by all the Jewish rabbis and by Maimonides upon the Jewish nation to keep silence upon everything relating to their cosmogony evinces a secret they are not willing should be known. The secret, therefore, explains itself to be that when the Jews were in captivity in Babylon and Persia they became acquainted with the cosmogony of the Persians, as registered in the Zend-Avesta of Zoroaster, the Persian lawgiver, which after their return from captivity they manufactured and modeled as their own, and antedated it by giving to it the name of Moses. The case admits of no other explanation. From all which it appears that the Book of Genesis, instead of being *the oldest book in the world*, as the Bishop calls it, has been the last written book of the Bible, and that the cosmogony it contains has been manufactured." (Reply to the Bishop of Llandaff, pp. 256, 257.)

Who can say, without quibbling, that such criticism is not destructive of the very foundations of the Christian's faith and hope?

Voltaire and the Deists of his time and Paine used these criticisms for this very purpose. Paine said: "But if it should be found that the books ascribed to Moses, Joshua, and Samuel were not written by Moses, Joshua, and Samuel, every part of the authority and authenticity of these books is gone at once; for there can be no such thing as forged or invented testimony." (Age of Reason, p. 79.)

Ingersoll uses the same criticisms with which to point the shafts he hurls at Christianity.

The Deists of Europe in the last century, of whom Lord Bolingbroke was the moving spirit and Voltaire the spokesman, in their brilliant and persistent warfare upon Christianity relied chiefly upon these criticisms to destroy faith in the Bible as the Word of God and bring the Christian religion into contempt, as infidels have ever done. As a result France plunged into infidelity and atheism, and the French Revolution, with its "Reign of Terror," followed.

In 1864 the late Earl of Beaconsfield (Disraeli), in addressing the diocesan convention at Oxford, England, said:

"The opinions of the new school are paralyzing the efforts of many who ought to be our friends. Will these opinions succeed? My opinion is that they will fail. * * * Having examined all their writings, I believe, without exception, whether they consist of fascinating eloquence, diversified learning, or picturesque sensibility exercised by our honored preacher in this university (Dean Stanley), and whom to know is to admire and regard; or whether you find them in the cruder conclusions of prelates who appear to have commenced their theological studies after they have grasped the crosier (Bishop Colenso); or whether I read the lucubrations of nebulous professors (Frederick Maurice), who, if they could persuade the public to read their writings, would go far to realize that eternal punishment which they deny; or, lastly, whether it be the provincial arrogance and precipitate self-complacency which flash and fire in an essay or review, I find the common characteristic of their writings is this—that their learning is always secondhand. * * * When I examine the writings of their masters, the great scholars of Germany, I find that in their labors also there is nothing new. All that inexorable logic, irresistible rhetoric, bewildering wit could avail to popularize these views was set in motion to impress the new learning on the minds of the two leading nations of Europe (by the English and French deistical writers of the last century), and they produced their effect (in the French Revolution). When the turbulence was over, when the waters had subsided, the sacred heights of Sinai and Calvary were again revealed; and amidst the wreck of thrones, extinct nations, and abolished laws mankind, tried by so many sorrows, purified by so much suffering, and wise with such unprecedented experience, bowed again before the divine truths that Omnipotence had intrusted to the custody and promulgation of a chosen people."

Without doubt England would have gone as did France but for the sweeping, wonderful, and glorious revivals under the lead of George Whitefield, John and Charles Wesley, and their colaborers, growing out of the so-called "Oxford Movement."

We all know that irreparable harm has been done the Christian religion by Paine, Ingersoll, their associates and followers. We also know how they used the same criticisms with which to poison the shafts hurled at Christianity.

The unspiritual condition of the churches (and it is lamentable when viewed in the light of the Reformation and its legitimate results) and the alarmingly prevalent skepticism, infidelity, and atheism among the masses of the people in Germany, Switzerland, and Holland is, without doubt, almost wholly attributable to the advocacy of these criticisms by a large majority of the prominent pastors and theological professors in those lands.

The same condition of affairs is measurably true in England, Scotland, New England, and in every community where this criticism is believed by any very considerable number of people and openly advocated. Show me a church the pastor of which believes and preaches these criticisms, and the members of which pretty generally accept them, and

I will show you a church that is worldly, formal, and unaggressive in spiritual work.

· In view of the above facts, is it possible that anyone can believe that these criticisms will promote the spiritual interests of the Church and be for the glory of God if advocated by such splendid and noble gentlemen as Drs. Driver, Briggs, and Harper? We know that it will not, because we know it cannot. Will not their high professions, unsullied characters, and commanding influence make this teaching all the more dangerous? We are very sure it will. Already it has made its way where infidel or rationalist could not possibly carry it, and is, therefore, working all the greater mischief.

These criticisms are taught in many theological seminaries and pulpits of orthodox churches of our land. They are being pushed to the fore in many of our Church papers and magazines. They are in the course of Bible study prepared by the American Institute of Sacred Literature, which course has been recommended to the Christian Endeavor societies of the world by their honored President, Dr. F. E. Clark. They may be found in many of the lesson helps used in Sunday schools all over the land. They find a place in the teaching at the Chautauqua assemblies almost everywhere. Brethren, claiming to believe the Bible is the Word of God, are pushing these criticisms everywhere they can with a zeal deserving a better cause.

It is a very common saying of the Supernaturalists that though there are numerous errors, discrepancies, and contradictions in the Bible, these in no sense imperil or jeopardize the doctrinal teachings of the book. Of course, to superficial thinkers this saying will appear specious; but to thoughtful, honest, and reverent souls fallacious and dangerous.

If the Bible contains historic, scientific, and chronological errors, on what ground can it be consistently argued that it is infallible in its doctrinal deliverances? If Jesus Christ and the inspired apostles were not competent and trustworthy authorities in matters of authorship of the Old Testament writings, by what parity of reasoning can one consistently appeal to their testimony in matters of doctrine? The fact is, men will not accept the doctrinal teachings of the book as infallible if they are led to believe that it is untrustworthy in other matters. Personally, I am confronted by this fact almost every day in my work. It is not an infrequent thing for me to meet young people in their "teens," the children of Christians, who put aside the claims of the Bible with a flippancy that is almost paralyzing and a *sang-froid* that is characteristic of a professional infidel by saying: "Professors Briggs and Harper and the best scholars in the Churches acknowledge that the Bible is full of errors and contradictions. Why, then, should I accept it as true?" I find this condition of affairs alarmingly upon the increase.

The learned Bishop Ryle recently said:

"It is vain to shut our eyes to the fact that a general miasma of unbelief seems to fill the air in this day. Our Lord's words are verified, 'When the Son of man cometh, shall he find faith on the earth?'" Archbishop Tait said, in dying words: "The age is becoming skeptical." Archbishop Thompson said: "The infidelity of the day is not only aggressive, it is omnipresent. It is found in the club and in the drawing room. It works in magazines, newspapers, and novels." A great Northern divine told the General Assembly of the Church of Scotland last June: "Agnosticism and materialism have become the fashion. The great reviews and magazines are full of it. Young misses fresh from school, and who are not sound on the multiplication table, will lisp to you that they are not sound in the faith. Young boys will tell you that they go in for agnosticism, a word of which they hardly know the meaning and which they would find it hard to spell."

These critics are sowing to the wind; the Church will reap the whirlwind. If the Church accepts their teachings and conclusions, then shall she be swept from her anchorage to drift with the whirling currents of agnosticism and skepticism, or be dashed upon the rocks of apostasy. May God help his people to cry mightily to him for deliverance from this imminent peril!

CHAPTER XVII.
SCHOLARSHIP.

Dr. B. W. Bacon, in an article in a recent issue of The Independent, says:

Prof. Briggs's challenge in The Presbyterian Review for April, 1887, to name one solitary professor in this department in all the Protestant universities of the continent of Europe who would consent on this "question" to be classed with Prof. Green, was reiterated by Prof. George T. Ladd, D.D., of Yale, in his "What is the Bible?" and by myself in "The Genesis of Genesis." It has been made far more explicit in Prof. Briggs's "Bible, Church, and Reason," by the enumeration *seriatim*, in an appendix, entitled, "Who are the Higher Critics?" of eighteen foremost Protestant universities of Germany, with their forty-eight chairs of Old Testament science; sixteen similar institutions of the rest of the Continent, with their thirty-three professors of the subject; seven of the principal universities and theological schools of Great Britain, with their twelve professorships; fourteen of the corresponding institutions of America, with their eighteen professors and thirty-five independent scholars of note, all of whom in their writings, as cited by title, present a "solid phalanx against the traditional theory."

To make this challenge still more explicit Prof. Briggs enumerates the exceptions, of which there are *none*, to his knowledge, on the Continent:

"The professors of Oxford, Cambridge, and Edinburgh are united in their support of the four documents. There is not an Old Testament professor of standing in Great Britain who takes any other view, except the venerable Principal Douglas, of Glasgow, who has recently resigned his chair. The majority of Old Testament professors in America are of the same opinion. The notable exceptions are Profs. W. H. Green, Howard Osgood, and E. C. Bissell."

Letters of inquiry dispatched the past week to the most eminent professors in this department at Yale, Andover, Johns Hopkins, and Chicago, have added, indeed, quite a number of names to Prof.

Briggs's list of one hundred and forty-six; but as to the three exceptions, now reduced by the lamented death of Prof. Bissell to two they have produced only expressions of wonder as to where Prof. Green would look for opposing authority, and of ignorance of its existence. Until The Independent shall have taken a census of authorities on "the Pentateuch question" the opponents of the documentary theory, besides Profs. Green and Osgood and the very few who, with Principal Cave, in England, and Prof. W. K. Beecher, of Auburn, N. Y., try to combine a documentary theory of Genesis, in whole or in part, with Mosaic authorship, must be classed as "great unknowns."

Prof. Briggs says:

The critical analysis of the Hexateuch is the result of more than a century of profound study of the documents by the greatest critics of the age. There has been a steady advance until the present position of agreement has been reached, in which Jew and Christian, Roman Catholic and Protestant, Rationalist and Evangelical scholars, Reformed and Lutheran, Presbyterian and Episcopalian, Unitarian, Methodist, and Baptist all concur. The analysis of the Hexateuch into several distinct original documents is a purely literary question, in which no article of faith is involved. Whoever, in these times, in the discussion of the literary phenomena of the Hexateuch, appeals to the ignorance and prejudice of the multitude, as if there were any peril to the faith in these processes of higher criticism, risks his reputation for scholarship by so doing. There are no Hebrew professors on the continent of Europe, so far as I know, who deny the literary analysis of the Pentateuch into four great documents (J, E, P, and D). The professors of Hebrew in the universities of Oxford, Cambridge, and Edinburgh, and tutors in a large number of theological colleges, hold the same opinion. A very considerable number of Hebrew professors of America are in accord with them. There are, indeed, a few professional scholars who hold to the traditional opinion, but these are in a hopeless minority. I doubt whether there is any question of scholarship whatever in which there is greater agreement among scholars than in this question of the literary analysis of the Hexateuch.

These are bold declarations indeed. I think them audacious assumptions. One hundred and forty-six persons and "a few professional scholars who hold to the traditional opinion" are all the scholars in Christendom who are entitled to have an opinion and competent to speak on these matters! It reminds me of the gentleman who said, "There is but one Greek scholar in this country, and modesty forbids my naming him." Of the one hundred and forty-six persons named, Prof. Lampe has shown that thirty-four of them do not belong to the classification made by Prof. Briggs; that five are Unitarians, and seventeen are unorthodox Jews. Of course, if this be "a purely literary question," other things being equal, the testimony of a Unitarian, a rationalist, a deist, or an infidel is of as much value as that of a devout Christian scholar; but, while it is true there is a literary phase to this question, it is transcended immeasurably by other considerations.

Prof. Lampe names forty-five scholars as favoring the traditional view. This number can be increased into the hundreds, if not thousands. There are great numbers of pastors, and not a few laymen, who are seldom if ever heard of outside their limited fields of labor—quiet, unassuming, studious men—who keep abreast of all the work of specialists in all departments of textual, historical, and analytical criticisms of the Bible; who read the Hebrew, Greek, and other ancient languages, and who are familiar with all that has been accomplished by the philologist and archæologist, who are just as competent to testify upon these matters as the one hundred and forty-six gentlemen mentioned by Prof. Briggs.

To read the bold claims of these professors one would think, if they did not know better, that biblical learning would die with them. And yet they might all die this day, and before sundown their chairs could all be filled a dozen times over by "traditionalists" as learned as they from among the pastors of churches in America.

It is a fact that all orthodox Jews are "traditionalists." Are none of them competent to speak upon the Hexateuchal question?

I have no doubt but that there is as much real learning among the clergy of the Roman Catholic Church as can be found in all Protestantism. An "Encyclical," recently issued by Pope Leo XIII, contains the following deliverance:

> The Sacred Books have been written in their entirety and in all their parts at the dictation of the Holy Spirit; and so far is it from being possible for an error to occur in what has been divinely inspired, that of itself inspiration not only excludes all error, but excludes and rejects it with the same necessity that renders it impossible for God, the Supreme Truth, to be the author of any error whatsoever.

This officially commits the whole Roman Catholic Church to a position of antagonism to the Higher Criticism.

In accordance with the authority conferred upon them by a Council of the Bishops of the American Protestant Episcopal Church, held in New York last October, a committee of bishops, consisting of John Williams, Bishop of Connecticut and presiding bishop; William Creswell Doane, Bishop of Albany; F. D. Huntington, Bishop of Central New York; William E. McLaren, Bishop of Chicago; George F. Seymour, Bishop of Springfield; and Henry C. Potter, Bishop of New York, have issued a pastoral letter to the clergy and laity throughout the country.

It is an unusual and extraordinary occasion that calls forth an address on the part of the American episcopate to the Church at large, and the reasons for the present letter are thus set forth in the introductory page:

> We, your bishops, having been assembled to take order, under the guidance of the Holy Ghost, for the extension of the kingdom of God, have availed ourselves of the opportunity to meet in council to consider our duty in view of certain novelties of opinion and expression, which have seemed to us to be subversive of the fundamental verities of Christ's religion. It has come to our knowledge that the minds of many of the faithful clergy and laity are disturbed and distressed by these things; and we desire to comfort them by the firm assurance that the episcopate of the Church, to which, in a peculiar manner, the deposit of faith has been intrusted, is not unfaithful to that sacred charge, but will guard and keep it with all diligence, as men who shall hereafter give account to God.

The address treats of "The Incarnation of Our Lord Jesus Christ" and "The Inspiration of the

Holy Scriptures." In concluding the discussion of the latter the bishops thus speak:

> The minute and reverent study of the divine Word must always be necessary and will always be profitable. The time will never come when men will not be obliged to combine the separate portions of God's Word, to study the fashions in which they were given, and to consider the operation of the Holy Ghost, both in and through the sacred writers; and the time will never come when the honest student of God's Word will not require and will not welcome every critical appliance which the providence of God may furnish, to cast new light on the sacred page. It would be faithless to think that the Christian religion has anything to fear from the critical study of the Holy Scriptures.
>
> We devoutly thank God for the light and truth which have come to us through the earnest labors of devout critics of the sacred text. What we deprecate and rebuke is the irreverent rashness and unscientific method of many professed critics, and the presumptuous superciliousness with which they vaunt erroneous theories of the day as established results of criticism. From this fault professedly Christian critics are not always exempt; and by Christian critics we mean those who, both by theory and practice, recognize the inspiration of God as the controlling element of Holy Scripture.

After asserting that no discovery of modern research, positively ascertained, is of a character to unsettle a Christian's faith in any particular, the letter continues:

> Any instruction or any study which makes any part of the Bible less authoritative than it really is, which weakens faith in its inspiration, which tends to eliminate Christ from the utterances of the prophets, or which leads a man to think of miracles with a half-suppressed skepticism, is a pernicious instruction and a pernicious study.

This "pastoral letter" commits the Protestant Episcopal Church also against the criticism condemned in these pages. I know there are some scholars in this branch of the Church of God who are advocating destructive methods of biblical criticism, hence this "pastoral." But the authorities condemn their views and work, and the scholarship of this denomination of Christians is in sympathy with these condemnatory views.

We all know how emphatically the Presbyterian Church, through its last three General Assemblies, has declared in favor of the traditional views as against those advocated by Prof. Briggs. After Prof. Briggs and the very few scholars in the Presbyterian Church who are one with him in this matter, is Prof. W. Henry Green, the only scholar belonging to this communion?

Not a single Orthodox Church has approved and adopted the conclusions of the Higher Criticism. Every Orthodox Church is committed to the traditional views. And yet these few men, assuming to possess well-nigh all the learning in Christendom, are demanding of the Church of God that she shall abandon views that are consistent and made precious by hallowed associations; that were baptized by the tears and blood of thousands "of whom the world was not worthy;" views that were the result of the labors of the Church's greatest scholars for twenty centuries; and for what? Assumptions, suppositions, conjectures, and no end of unprovable opinions.

These gentlemen are creating a literature wholly

their own; and, with a zeal worthy of a better cause, are pushing it into the theological seminaries and the libraries of pastors all over the civilized world. They are making a lexicon, so that their own definitions may become current, and are translating the Bible to suit their own private interpretations. The immediate evil accomplished by them is not great, since their audience is small. Their writings are too dry, hair-splitting, and voluminous ever to become popular; but the ultimate evil may be very great, since the young men they are impressing with their views are to go abroad in the Church and world and sow broadcast the seeds of error; and, as rationalism and infidelity were the natural and inevitable harvest of the sowing of Baur and the Tübingen school in the Protestant Churches of continental Europe, so will it be in Great Britain and America fifty years hence if they succeed in accomplishing their purposes.

These critics tell us that their criticisms will not disturb the doctrines of the Bible; that they are only clearing away the rubbish that we may see these doctrines in a clearer and better light. Prof. Emil Schurer, of Kiel, insists that the doctrines of the Bible are in no danger; and yet, in the second paragraph from the one in which this view is expressed, he tells of a theological revolution already accomplished by the Higher Critics.

We know how extensive and influential were the influences of the Higher Criticism in unspiritualizing the Protestant Churches of Germany, Switzerland, and Holland. Wellhausen himself tells us how he left the theological faculty at Greifswald of his own accord in the consciousness of no longer standing quite on the basis of the Evangelical Church and Protestantism. Hengstenberg has well said: "The denial of the Pentateuch has its origin in the proneness to Naturalism, which has its root in estrangement from God."

But, will the work of these critics prevail? We know it will not.

The inspired Psalmist said: "Thou hast magnified thy Word above all thy name." We see this in its literary and poetic beauty; in its historic, scientific, and biographical accuracy; in its ethical and philosophical profundity; in its indestructibleness and elevating and transforming power; and in its prophetic and eschatological uniqueness. The Written Word tells of the Living Word—tells of him who created all things; who is the "Light of the world" and Saviour of men. God gave him "the name which is above every name." The greatness and glory of this name shall be recognized and acknowledged by all created intelligences, in heaven, in earth, and under the earth; and, at last "every tongue shall confess that Jesus Christ is Lord, to the glory of God the Father." The names of rulers, warriors, and statesmen; of philosophers, scientists, and theologians; of critics, skeptics, and infidels, great, noble, and illustrious in the sight and estimation of men, will pale as the morning star before the rising sun before the name of Jesus. And yet God has magnified his Word, by which he made the heavens, and which "endureth forever," above this greatest and most glorious of names. Surely that which God has so exalted and honored we do well and wisely to love, cherish, and obey. "For we can do nothing against the truth, but for the truth" (2 Cor. 13:8).

CHAPTER XVIII.

CONTROVERSY.

There are many in the Church of God who are averse to controversy. Some of them are gentle, quiet, timid, shrinking souls, who cannot understand the martial commands and exhortations of the Bible. Others are trimmers and politicians — "peace-at-any-price" people. They will not censure or condemn the man who destroys the "Old Faith" if he claims to be a supernaturalist; but, strangely enough, they decry and condemn the man who defends it. Hence the critics who claim to believe the Bible is the Word of God are almost unhindered in pushing their rationalistic work and views. These people oppose the work of infidels; they condemn the destructive criticisms of the acknowledged rationalists; but, when a man in the Church, professing to believe the Bible to be a supernatural revelation of the mind and will of God, does the very same work, these people insist that they must not be opposed, and will condemn as unloving and unchristlike the man who does it.

They say, "We do not want controversy; we want peace." They seem not to know that God's Word says, "First pure, then peaceable" (James 3:17). It is utterly impossible to have peace in the Church excepting upon the ground of loyalty to God's Word. Jesus said, "I came not to send peace, but a sword" (Matt. 10:34). This is all "because the mind of the flesh is enmity against God" (Rom. 8:7). God commands the Christian teacher to "reprove them sharply, that they may be sound in the faith, not giving heed to" the "commandments of men who turn away from the truth" (Titus 1:13, 14). Timothy was commanded to "Reprove, rebuke, exhort, with all long-suffering and teaching. For the time will come" (without doubt here now) "when they will not endure the sound doctrine" (the integrity and sufficiency of the Old Testament Scriptures, see Chap. 3); but, having itching ears, will heap to themselves teachers after their own lusts; and will turn away their ears from the truth, and turn aside unto fables" (2 Tim. 4:2-4).

In the Introduction to "Anti-Higher Criticism" (Hunt & Eaton, 150 Fifth Avenue, New York) I characterized some of the work of some of the critics as "audacious assumptions." One prominent Church paper called the use of such language "unscholarly and unchristlike." The reviewer did not say my statement was untrue. If it were untrue, of course it would have been "unscholarly and unchristlike." But it is true. Can the truth be unscholarly and unchristlike? The effort to make it appear that one is "unscholarly and unchristlike" because he tells the unvarnished truth is an acknowledgment of the weakness of their cause, and would not be made only because of those in the

Church who are afraid to call "a spade a spade" and the "Peace-at-any-price" party.

What of the language of the Saviour when, in speaking to the Scribes and Pharisees, who "made void the word of God because of their traditions?" (Matt. 15:6, R. V.) He called them "hypocrites;" "ye serpents, ye offspring of vipers" (Matt. 23:33); and "liars" (John 8:55); etc., etc.

Was Paul "unscholarly and unchristlike" when, in speaking to one who sought to "turn aside the proconsul from the faith," he said to him: "O, full of all guile and all villainy, thou son of the devil, thou enemy of all righteousness, wilt thou not cease to pervert the right ways of the Lord?" (Acts 13:10.)

Was the gentle, loving John "unscholarly and unchristlike" when he characterized as "liars" all who deny the deity of Jesus Christ (1 John 2:22); the man who claimed to be a Christian and yet will not obey God (1 John 2:4); and he who "hateth his brother" (1 John 4:20)?

Away with that sentimentalism and cowardice that apologizes for one, or condemns him, for telling the truth and calling things by their right names about the work and views of those who are undermining the fortress of the Church of Jesus Christ!

While we ought to love these men personally, and do them all the good we can (and I am sure I do and will, and I have never said or written one word derogatory of them personally), at the same time we must condemn their destructive work or become party to it. (2 John 9-11.)

These be perilous times. In addition to the prevailing unbelief there is an alarming increase of skepticism, rationalism, agnosticism, and infidelity. Can any one for a moment believe that the work of the Higher Critics will turn this tide in the right direction? We do know that their work is largely the cause of it.

Bishop Ryle says:

> And what is the source of all this mischief? I believe it is the result of the constant attacks made by the learned critics on the inspiration of the Old Testament, producing a general feeling of skepticism about the New among the large mass of people who know nothing of any criticism, but are glad of some excuse for doubting the truth of the whole Bible. The consequence is a general shakiness in men's minds about Bible religion altogether. I firmly believe that many of our modern critics mean no harm, but actually think they are doing God service. But I believe with equal firmness that one result of this Higher Criticism is that many people in this day never read their Bibles at all, or at any rate read less than they used to.

CHAPTER XIX.

SOME NOTEWORTHY TESTIMONIES.

Josephus, the great Jewish historian, who wrote about A. D. 92, 93, says, concerning the canon of the Old testament:

"With us," in contrast to the contradictions of Greek history, "there are, not myriads of books inharmonious and conflicting, but two and twenty books only, containing the records of the whole time, and rightly believed to be Divine. Of these, five are those of Moses, which comprises as well the matters of law as the account of the generation of man, to the time of his death. This period is little short of 3,000 years. But from the death of Moses to the reign of Artaxerxes, the King of Persia after Xerxes, the prophets after Moses wrote what was done in their times, in thirteen books. The four remaining books contain hymns to God, and suggestions to men as to their lives. From Artaxerxes down to our own times, events have been recorded, but they have not been accounted worthy of the same credit as those before them, because the exact succession of Prophets existed no longer. And it is evident indeed, how we stand affected by our own writings. For, so long a period having now elapsed, no one has dared either to add or to take away from them, or to change any thing; it being a thing implanted in all the Jews from their birth, that they should account them as oracles of God, and abide by them, and, if needful to gladly die for them."

He further says:

"Since I see many attending to the blasphemies uttered by some out of hostility, and disbelieving what I have written about our antiquities, and making it a token of the modernness of our race, that the celebrated Grecian historians have not accounted it worthy of mention, I thought it needful to write briefly of all these things."

Professor Luthardt can speak from experience on this subject. For nearly 40 years he has been professor of theology, at Leipsic, and an effective leader among the evangelical scholars of Germany. He has combatted the rationalistic theories that were so popular and threatening a generation ago, and he has lived to see them dead and buried. Therefore he has no anxiety because of the new storms that have arisen. In a recent article he utters these encouraging words:

"We have had too many experiences in this respect, have seen too many hypotheses come and go. Who knows what gravediggers already stand at the door? We older ones had experience in Baur's criticism of the New Testament, and some of us took an active part in opposing it. Where is that school now? What a stir D. F. Strauss made in his day! All who understand the matter now have abandoned the theory that the life of Jesus consists of myths. How many in Germany, even in scientific circles, compromised themselves by their attitude towards Renan's Life of Jesus! Who ever speaks seriously of this French romance now?"

Coleridge remarks:

"One striking proof of the genuineness of the Mosaic Books is this: they contain precise prohibitions, by way of predicting the consequences of disobedience, of all those things which David and Solomon actually did and gloried in doing—raising cavalry, making a treaty with Egypt, laying up treasure, and polygamizing. Now, could such prohibitions have been fabricated in these kings' reigns or afterwards? Impossible!"

Kiel and Delitzsch in Introduction to Genesis say:

"All that has been adduced as proof of the contrary (the Mosaic origin) by the so-called Modern Criticism, is founded either upon misunderstanding and misinterpretation, or upon a misapprehension of the peculiarities of the Semitic style of historical writing, or lastly, upon doctrinal prejudices, in other words, upon a repudiation of all the supernatural characteristics of Divine revelation, whether in the form of miracle or prophecy."

Rawlinson, the distinguished antiquarian and one of the most competent of critics, says:

Every work which comes down to us as the work of a particular author, is to be accepted as his production, unless strong grounds can be produced to the contrary. The *onus probandi* lies with the person who denies the genuineness; and, unless the arguments adduced in proof are very weighty, the fact of reputed authorship ought to overpower them. Sound criticism has generally acquiesced in this canon. It raises an important presumption in favor of the Mosaic authorship of the Pentateuch, anterior to any proof of the fact to be derived from internal evidence, or from the testimony of those who had special opportunities of knowing. . . . . Until it is shown that the book was not composed by its reputed author, the mode and time of its composition are not fit objects of research. . . . There is really not a pretence for saying that recent discoveries in the field of history, monumental or other, have made the acceptance of the Mosaic narrative in its plain and literal sense any more difficult now, than in the days of Bossuet and Stillingfleet.

To the charge of Dewette, that the evidence for the Pentateuch is of little worth, because the Jews were *uncritical*, he says: "The Jews and Greeks, who during eighteen centuries, without a dissentient voice, ascribed the 'Book of the Law' to Moses, were not acquainted with the modern Critical Analysis, which claims to be an infallible judge of the age, and mode of composition, of every literary production. It is true the witnesses include apostles, prophets, confessors, our Blessed Lord Himself; but the distance of these witnesses is held to invalidate their testimony; or if the words of One at least are too sacred to be gainsaid, He spoke (it is argued) by way of accommodation, in order not to shock the prejudices of the Jew. . .

"It appears that the Pentateuch is either cited or mentioned as the work of Moses, by almost the whole series of Jewish historical writers from Moses to Ezra.

Rev. Mason Gallagher, in "Modern Objections— Antiquated Errors," calls attention to the celebrated case of the critic Leclerc or Clericus, as follows:

In the last century the celebrated critic Leclerc or Clericus, was led to deny that the Pentateuch was the genuine work of Moses, on grounds similar to those now ventilated.

Dr. Dick in his admirable Lectures on Theology, p. 27, Am. Ed., says of Leclerc: "His hypothesis is conjectural, improbable, and contrary not only to the uniform belief of the whole Jewish nation, but also to the testimony of inspiration." He then refers to the reply of Witsius to Leclerc, and quotes Watson's Apology, Letter III. "A small addition to a book," it has been observed, "does not destroy the genuineness or the authenticity of the whole book." He thus continues: "It is probable that Clericus hastily adopted this opinion: it is certain that on mature reflection he renounced it, and acquiesced in the common belief of Jews and Christians, which is confirmed by the testimony of our Lord and His Apostles, that the first five books of the Bible were written by Moses." (See Prolegom. 1 Dissert. III, Scriptore Pentateuchi.)

The experience of Leclerc is so interesting in this connection that we are led to give an extract from the "Jews' Letter to Voltaire," who, when this arch-infidel used the name of this great German critic, to fortify his attacks on Moses, replied: "We shall not conceal that Leclerc did at first hold this opinion. But if we owed that acknowledgement to truth, were you not under the same obligation to inform your readers, that he changed his mind since, and in a riper age openly embraced that opinion which he combatted in his youth?" Leclerc says: "These slight additions, made by the prophets who lived after Moses, ought not to prevent us from looking upon him as the author of the Pentateuch, since there are so many other proofs of this, just as the Hebrew antiquities are ascribed to Josephus, although some passages may have been inserted by recent hands;" and again: " Moses cannot with any show of reason, be denied to have been the real author of the Pentateuch." (See Jews' Letters to Voltaire, p. 145–7.)

The late very scholarly Dr. Liddon, Canon of St. Paul's, said:

For Christians it will be enough to know that our Lord Jesus Christ set the seal of His infallible sanction on the whole of the Old Testament. He found the Hebrew canon as we have it in our hands to-day, and He treated it as an authority which was above discussion. Nay, more; He went out of His way—if we may reverently speak thus—to sanction not a few portions of it which modern skepticism rejects.

Thus, to take an example: In the Book of Deuteronomy long addresses are ascribed to Moses (Deut. i, 1, etc.; v, 1, etc.), and Moses describes a series of events of which he claims to have been an eye-witness (Deut. ix. 16; x. 1–5, etc). If, then, we are told that the addresses were really unspoken and these events unwitnessed by Moses; that the "dramatized" or, to speak plainly, fictitious account of them was composed by some Jew, with a fine idealizing faculty, who lived many centuries after Moses; and this, although the book was undoubtedly imposed upon the conscience of the Jewish people, at any rate after the exile, as the work of Moses himself ; we must observe that such a representation is irreconcilable with the veracity of the book, which by its use of the name of the great law-giver claims an authority that, according to the critics in question, does not belong to it; or, if that striking prediction in the eighth chapter of the Book of Daniel, about King Antiochus Epiphanes (Dan. viii, 13–25), was really, as has been asserted, written after the events referred to, and thrown into the form of prediction by some scribe of the second century before Christ, in order to arouse and encourage the Jews in their long struggle with the Græco-Syrian power, then it must be said that the book in which it occurs is not trustworthy; the writer is endeavoring to produce a national enthusiasm by means of a representation which he must have known to be contrary to fact.

Are we to suppose that in these and other (St. John v. 46, 47; *cf.* Deut. xviii, 15, 18, etc.), references to the Old Testament our Lord was only using *ad hominem* arguments, or talking down to the level of a popular ignorance which He did not Himself share? Not to point out the inconsistency of this supposition with His character as a perfectly sincere religious teacher, it may be observed that in the Sermon on the Mount He marks off those features of the popular Jewish religion which He rejects (St. Matt. v. 27-48) or modifies, in a manner which makes it certain that, had He not Himself believed in the historic truth of the events and persons to which He thus refers, He would have said so. But did He then share a popular belief which our higher knowledge has shown to be popular ignorance? and was He whom His apostle believed to be full of grace and truth (St. John i, 14) and "in whom are hid all the treasures of wisdom and knowledge" (Col. ii, 3), indeed mistaken as to the real worth of those Scriptures to which He so often and so confidently appealed? There are those who profess to bear the Christian name, and yet do not shrink from saying as much as this. But they will find it difficult to persuade mankind that, if He could be mistaken on a matter of such strictly religious importance as the value of the sacred literature of His countrymen He can be safely trusted about any thing else. The trustworthiness of the Old Testament is, in fact, inseparable from the trustworthiness of our Lord Jesus Christ; and if we believe that He is the true Light of the world, we shall close our ears against suggestions impairing the credit of those Jewish Scriptures which have received the stamp of His divine authority.

Prof. Taylor Lewis in his Introduction to Genesis in Lang's Commentary, says:

Those who set the least value on the idea of inspiration, find a fancied support not only of what is called the documentary theory of Genesis, but also of their favorite notion of earlier and later periods in the composition of the whole and even of particular parts. . . . This view is already curing itself by its ultra-rationalistic extravagance. It reduces Old Testament Scriptures not only to fragments, but to fragments of fragments in most ill-assorted and jumbled confusion. Its supporters find themselves, at last, in direct opposition to their favorite maxim, that the Bible must be interpreted as though written like any other book. For, surely, no other book was ever so composed or so compiled. In the same narrative, presenting every appearance of narrative unity, they find the strangest juxtaposition of passages from different authors, and written at different times, according as the one name (Elohim) or the other (Jehovah) is found in it. One verse, and even a clause of a verse, is written by the Elohist, the next by the Jehovist, with nothing besides this difference of names to mark any difference in purpose or authorship. Calling it a compilation will not help the absurdity, for no other compilation was ever made in this way. To make the confusion worse, there is brought in, occasionally, a third or a fourth writer, or an editor, or reviewer, and all this without any of those actual proofs or tests, which are applied to other ancient writings, and in the use of which this "Higher Criticism," as it calls itself, is so much inclined to vaunt.

Principal Cave, in his "Battle of the Standpoints" bears the following testimony:

"Genesis, we aver, is a compilation of *two* documents, an Elohist and Jehovist document," said the Decomposition Critics about the beginning of this century. But it was objected, no mere compilation could have produced such a book. "Allow us to amend our theory," replied the Critics, "and permit us to say, that Genesis, so far from being a mere compilation of *two* works, is a new and much enlarged edition of *one* man's work (the Elohist) by another (the Jehovist)." But it was objected to this, why speak you of Genesis only, why do you not extend the process to all the Books of the Law? "Why not, indeed?"

replied the Critics. "Allow us to amend our theory again, and say that the whole Law, as well as Genesis, is the result of *supplementing*, by the Jehovist, of the document of the Elohist." But again it was objected, that so uniform a book as Deuteronomy could not have been the product of such a process. "You are quite right," said the Critics, "we will again amend our theory and say, now, that the *Pentateuch* is a *supplementing* by the Jehovist, of *two* original works written, one by the Elohist, the other by the Deuteronomist." But it was further objected, that the sections attributed to the Jehovist sometimes contained the *name* of Elohim, and sometimes showed the *style* of the Elohist. "Again you are right," rejoined the Critics "we will once more amend our theory, and say that there are *two Elohistic* documents, an earlier and a later." But to this it was still objected that perhaps the order of writing is *not* Elohist, Deuteronomist, Jehovist. "There is no 'perhaps' about it," said the Critics; "allow us the goodness to amend again; we now desire to consider that writer as the latest whom we held formerly to be the earliest, and we now declare the order of writing to be Jehovist, Deuteronomist, Elohist." But it was objected, again, that there are facts which do not square with this view. "We will, therefore," said the Critics, "amend again our theory. Manifestly it is too simple. Let us make it more complicated, and express our belief that the Jehovist shows traces of at least *three hands*, and the Deuteronomist of *three hands*, and the Elohist of *three hands*." But it was again objected, that if the Elohist wrote the "Book of Law" about B. C. 400, then it is impossible to explain how Elohistic terms and practices could occur in the "Book of Joshua," written, say, about B. C. 1400. "Oh!" said the Decomposition Critics, "we affirm that the Book of Joshua was not written prior to B. C. 400." But it was objected that there are Psalms expressly attributed to David, and yet in these Davidic Psalms, written, say, about B. C. 1000, there are evident references to the Elohistic sections of the Law, said to have been written *before* B. C. 400. "Really, under the exigencies of our theory," replied the Critics, "we will just deny that any Psalms whatever were written by David."

So spake the Critics. How amusing it would be, were it not so lamentable! The latest "*adjustment*" I know of comes from Dr. Kuenen. In the old edition of his *Introduction to the Old Testament*, Leyden, 1863, Dr. Kuenen dated the prophecy of Joel as about B. C. 860. But Joel contains references of an Elohistic kind, and consequently, in his edition, published last year, he says that Joel was written "*after*, rather than *before*, B. C. 400. Nor has Criticism, I imagine, finished its '*adjustments*' yet! Nay, I believe, with that talented man, Professor Strack, of Berlin, that, in spite of the great popularity which the views of Graf and Wellhausen enjoy at the present time, I am nevertheless persuaded that an essential change in the previous treatment of the history of Israel, and especially of the activity of Moses, will not exist permanently." Nay, I go further than Strack, for he somewhat qualifies this statement of his. In my view, Criticism, under the stress of Criticism, will presently complete the circle, and avow, as a further " *adjustment*," that *the Pentateuch was written by Moses after all!*—In his recent trenchant article on the " Old Testament and Its Critics," he writes : " I venture to impugn the judgment of the authorities (Wellhausen, Dillmann, Ewald, Dewette and others), and I do so after having some years ago, cordially, nay, enthusiastically, believed in their value. But maturer, and more protracted examination has led me utterly to distrust the more serious results announced by these authorities. While I cannot but express my warmest gratitude to the great German experts in the Old Testament, I feel myself reluctantly compelled to avow, that experience has led me to distrust the conclusions these experts have drawn from the facts they have so perseveringly marshalled." (Cont. Rev., April, 1890, 341, 3.)

Professor Green, in his reply to Professor Harper's presentation of the case, speaks as follows:

The serious aspect of the affair is this, that there are presuppositions involved in the arguments employed and deductions made, which are subversive of the credibility and inspired authority of the sacred record. This constitutes the gravity of the case, as it affects the great body of those who reverence the Scriptures as the Word of God. The mythical character attaching to the early records of pagan nations, is not to be imputed to the biblical account of the primæval age of the world, or of the origin of the Israelitish people, for the narrative of the Bible is absolutely unique. It stands alone, among all the records of antiquity, in preserving in its primitive purity the true knowledge of God, in its freedom from mythological conceits, and in presenting a truly rational account, strikingly confirmed in its main outlines at least, if not in all its details, by modern scientific research, as no similar document of antiquity can pretend to be, in relation to the Origin of the World, Unity of the Human Race, Primæval History of Mankind, and the filiation of the Nations. And, as a preliminary stage in a grand scheme of Divine Revelation continued through succeeding ages, whose reality and supernatural character are attested by the most convincing proofs, it has a well-founded claim to be regarded as transmitting a faithful account of God's dealings with men from the beginning.

"The laws, from Exodus to Deuteronomy, are, by their own positive claim, by ineffaceable internal indications, and by both the express attestation and incidental historical confirmation of subsequent Scriptures, irrefragically Mosaic. And Genesis, which is clearly preliminary to the books that follow, must, as the critics themselves allow, have the same origin as they. There is something clearly wrong in a 'Critical Process' which can take a history that, in itself, is quite consistent and entirely credible, and sunder it into distinct documents mutually repugnant and irreconcileable. A purely 'Literary Analysis' on grounds of diction, style, and modes of thought, cannot impair the truth of what is otherwise credible, or the consistency of what is in itself harmonious. And, in fact, the damaging consequences attributed to the critical hypothesis result in great part, from inferences resting not on positive data, but on the critics. The fundamental vice in the whole process is that they quietly assume what they undertake to demonstrate. When the credibility of Genesis is undermined, by alleging that the primary documents out of which it was complied were first committed to writing many centuries after the Mosaic age, this conclusion is notoriously and avowedly based on grounds which presuppose their unhistorical character, convert them into fluctuating myths and legends, and assume likewise that all the rest of the sacred history has been tampered with, and deliberately falsified. As to the Middle Books of the Pentateuch, the divisive hypothesis launches into the open sea, destitute of chart or compass," encountering "reefs, shallows, cross-currents, whirlpools, fogs and storms, and every peril known to navigators. If the History of Literature affords an ampler illustration of 'confusion worse confounded,' that the hopeless inextricable medley in which the critics find themselves in their attempts to struggle through the three middle books of the Pentateuch, and that acquisition of doubtful value to themselves which they use in order to create a Hexateuch, the Book of Joshua, it has never yet been discovered." And as to the argument from "Style," "Discrepancies," "Duplicate Accounts," "Contradictions," "Divine Name," etc., etc. "The discrepancies and contradictions alleged to prove diversity of authorship do not exist; if they did they would make the work of the Redactor inconceivable. There is no duplicate account of the Creation, nor of the line of the descent from Adam to the existing race of mankind, nor of the Deluge. There are no such differences of language as require the assumption of a diversity of writers. The alternation of the Divine Names can be explained without this assumption. The alleged difference of style is fictitious.

He concludes his masterly refutation of Prof. Harper's views, by saying:

"My own private opinion on the subject corresponds with that of Zophar the Naamathite, respecting the Saviourian hypothesis. When he would say, in the most emphatic manner, that a thing is impossible he says that it may take place 'when a wild ass's colt is born a man!' Job 2: 12."

The following very explicit testimony is by Prof. S. K. Kellogg:

Our Saviour took it for granted that the whole legislative part of the Pentateuch was the work of Moses; so that to my mind Christ has settled that question. But it does not follow, necessarily, and therefore, Moses with his own hand wrote every word of that law. Yet to many the teaching of our Lord as to the Mosaic authorship of the book of the law is not decisive. Some argue that it is possible that our Lord may have been ignorant on this matter, without any prejudice to His divinity. According to this unbelieving theory, when He thought He was quoting the Word of God to Moses, He was really quoting a priestly forgery; and this means that He was so ignorant of the meaning of the Father, that He did not know His Father's own word when He saw it.

Is it credible to any loyal Christian that His ignorance extended as far as this? I must say that if that was so, that Jesus was mistaken as to that, He might also have been mistaken as to His being the Son of God. The critics of the unbelieving school maintain, for instance, that the Law as given in the book of Deuteronomy only originated in the days of Josiah; but our Lord quotes from Deuteronomy as the law of Moses. You remember when the Sadduces asked about the widow who was to marry her deceased husband's brother, the Lord referred them to the law of Moses, and in particular to this book, the book of Deuteronomy. And in another place, our Saviour in John 5, said to the Jews, "If ye had believed Moses, ye would have believed me; but if ye believe not his writings, how shall ye believe My words?" Now, this appears to me conclusive, and I am convinced that in at least the general sense which I explained at first, when Christ spoke of the book in that general way He really endorsed it as in a true sense the law of Moses. All the force of His argument depends upon the fact that Moses " Wrote of Him;" and if these four words are true, then our Lord Jesus certifies not only to its authorship, but to its inspiration, for to write of Christ centuries before He came implies supernatural foreknowledge in the writer.

I have referred to the claim of Mosaic authorship of large parts of the Pentateuch which the work itself contains. In Leviticus, for example, fifty-six times in twenty-seven chapters it is stated or implied that this law was given by the Lord to Moses; fifty-six falsehoods, if the rationalists are right. Furthermore, the language of this law is not modern Hebrew. Then there are so many allusions, incidents, and regulations, which are perfectly natural if the Pentateuch was written in the time of the Exodus; but which are simply unaccountable if it was first originated at a later period. It is repeatedly evident that the writer had intimate knowledge of the Egyptian law, the customs and manners in the days of Moses; and it is almost impossible to believe that any man could have written the book so many centuries afterwards without error in some such minute details, which, indeed, he could have had no sufficient motive for inventing.

In the references which he makes he is always true to the facts as they were fifteen centuries before Christ. Archæological researches are also confirming this argument. In like manner, we have references to various customs of the Egyptians in that age; as, for instance, to the goat worship of Mendes; as in the Revised version in Lev. 17. And we find many references in the law to wilderness-life; as in laws for the "camp;" but what would be the object in inventing these when Israel had for centuries been settled in Canaan. It would only have increased the danger of detecting the forged character of the narrative to burden it with such details.

Again, if the law of Moses was written in Palestine long after Moses' day, the writer, whoever he was, in the law of clean and unclean animals, would have referred to the animals about him in Canaan, but instead he enumerated the animals of the Sinaitic Peninsula. Would a Palestinian writer command Israel not to eat many beasts that they had never seen?

Last of all, I cannot shut my eyes to the fact that in this book there are predictions. The 26th chapter of the book of Leviticus, is a marvellous miniature of Israel's history, and the book of Deuteronomy contains another. In these there are many details of Israel's history predicted, that were not fulfilled at the time, and are not fulfilled yet, but will be in the future. But these predictions cannot be forgeries; for they imply the inspiration of the writer by the Holy Ghost.

In the Lambeth Conference of 1888, composed of the Bishops of the Church of England and the Protestant Episcopal church:

A report was presented, in some respects the most able and masterly of all the reports offered; but after a discussion, the earnestness and solemnity of which could not fail to impress each member of this body, the report was re-committed by an overwhelming vote in consequence of a few expressions which seemed to convey the impression, or, at least, to take the position for the sake of argument, with the unbeliever, that the Church felt well assured only of the *substantial* truth of the New Testament; and further conceding, or seeming to concede, that the opening portions of the Word of God, like its close, were a vision or an allegory. The conclusions seemingly to be deduced from the few phrases we have indicated by this report, were denied by the members of the Committee; but the sense of the reverence due to the Word of God was such that no explanations were deemed sufficient to prevent the re-commitment of the whole report with a view to the elimination of its objectionable features. On its reappearance, with modifications in its language and expressions, at a later day, objection was still made to what was deemed unwise and unnecessary admissions, and finally the report, able and excellent in all but a few words, as it certainly was, was refused a place in the printed proceedings of the Conference by an overwhelming majority. This action of the assembled bishops affirmed their reverence and respect for the Word of God, and their unwillingness, even for argument's sake, to make concessions as to its substantial verity, or admissions that might characterize portions of it as vision or allegory. It was feared that the language of the report might be misunderstood, and its admissions might be used to detract from the confidence all should feel in God's Word as the revelation of his will and way.

No one who was present at this debate can fail to recall the earnest, scholarly and impressive speech of the learned Bishop of Gloucester and Bristol, Dr. Ellicott, in defense of the Bible—the whole Bible. Like solemn and eloquent words were spoken by the Bishops of Durham, Dr. Lightfoot; Winchester, Dr. Harold Browne; and Cork, Dr. Gregg. Every American bishop present, save one, voted for the re-commitment of the report.—*New York Independent, Nov.* 19, 1891.

The almost unanimous vote of the Presbyterian General Assembly, in Detroit, May 1891, refusing to approve the appointing Prof. Briggs to a chair in Union Theological Seminary, was fairly expressive of the views entertained by that great and learned body, of the " Higher Criticism," as expounded by Prof. Briggs.

The following named scholars, every one an intellectual giant, may be named, beside many I have already named, and many more that I might name, are against the Higher Criticism in its popular sense: Eichorn, Michaelis, Rosemuller, Neander, Tholuck, Ranke, Hengstenberg, Lange, Drechsler, Kiel and Havernick.

The following eloquent, earnest and spirited words were used by the scholarly Critic, Dr. Nathaniel West, in closing a most able and convincing address against the Higher Criticism at Mr. Moody's Conference, at Northfield, in the Summer of 1891:

I have gone through every argument they have in every writer that I can get hold of, and there are 100,000 men in this land who can read German just as well as these professors and understand it when translated into English, and know what it is just as well as I know it. The higher criticism rests on assumptions, presuppositions and postulates and inferences and deductions from false premises, all of which are subversive of the authority of both Testaments and destructive of the authority of the Lord Jesus Christ and His apostles in the Church.

We are not frightened, although we are aroused. If there is anything under heaven for which a man and woman ought to fight, it is that eternal truth of God, which was purchased by the blood of God's dear Son, baptized by the consecrating Spirit of His grace, and which, like incorruptible seed, is sown by the living God in the hearts of His people, there to germinate, bloom, and bring forth fruit in time and eternity. And wherever the Lord Jesus has a banner flying for that, you will find me there, with a sword, fighting, if it costs me life and everything. The time is come when I am obliged to make choice between smiling and shaking hands with my friends, and smiling and shaking hands with Jesus. "He that is not with Me is against Me;" and, when it comes to that, whether I shall let Jesus go and be silent about Him and His truth, or let my friend, the professor, go, I say to you, beloved professor, the choice is neither doubtful nor difficult.

The time is coming when that bright sun of to-day will gather blackness, and the moon will lose the sheen of her splendor and turn into blood, and the stars in the vault of heaven will disappear, and convulsions will shake this entire world. The three that glitter in the belt of Orion will pale away, and Alps and Apennines uprooted from their base will go dancing to plunge headlong into the Rockies rushing to meet them. But high over all the wreck of sublunary things, this Word of God, from Genesis to Revelation, shall stand, immortal, immovable, unchangeable, a monument of all the attributes of Father, Son and Holy Ghost, a testimony of love, and of grace, and of truth to His people now, and to His people hereafter. And I heard a voice saying to me, "Cry;" and I said, "What shall I cry?" The higher criticism is grass, and the goodness thereof is as the flower of the field. The grass withereth and the flower thereof fadeth. Why? "Because the Spirit of the Lord bloweth upon it." Surely the Higher Criticism is grass, but "the Word of our God shall stand forever."

Sir William Dawson, one of the most eminent scientists of our day, in a recent address to a band of theological students, among other good things said :

I have read recently, I confess with feelings of contempt, discussions respecting the supposed limitations of the knowledge of Jesus Christ. Did he know the data of Modern Criticism? Was he acquainted with the discoveries of modern science? The fly alighting on my hand might as well attempt to understand the thoughts passing through my mind as criticism to gauge in this way the mind of Christ. To me, as a student for fifty years of nature, of man, and of the Bible, such discussions seem most frivolous, since our Lord's knowledge, as we have it in his reported discourses, is altogether above and beyond our science and philosophy; transcending them as much as the vision of an astronomer, armed with one of the great telescopes of our time, transcends the unaided vision of a gnat. Christ views things from a standpoint of his own and through a different medium from the atmosphere of this world. His difficulty appears to be to convey heavenly thoughts to us through the imperfect language in which we speak of earthly thoughts.

That most eminent archæologist, Professor A. H. Sayce, recently said :

I do not think that the Higher Critics have established anything beyond the composite authorship of some of the books of the Bible. As regards their historical conclusions I am very much at issue with them. I think they have endeavored to demolish the history contained in the Old Testament upon most insufficient evidence, and in accordance with a method which could not and would not be applied to secular history, and I further believe that modern discoveries in Oriental archæology are re-establishing the history which the Higher Critics supposed they have demolished.

In a recent issue of the Contemporary Review, Prof. Sayce says:

Let me briefly review some of the reasons which preclude me from offering any longer the same welcome to the method and conclusions of the Higher Criticism that I was prepared to accord to them fifteen years ago. The pivot upon which the whole question turns is the Pentateuch, or the Hexateuch, as our critical friends would make it. If the Pentateuch is really a hodge-podge of ill-digested morsels, none of which is older than the age of the Jewish monarchy, while a considerable part of them is post-exilic, we may at once give up the contest, and follow our critical friends whithersoever they lead us. The Christian Church will have erred grievously like the Jewish Church before it, and the law which our Lord came to fulfill, instead of being the rock upon which the faith of Israel was founded, will have been the product of religious degeneracy and decay. Moses will vanish, no man knoweth where, like his sepulchre in the land of Moab, and the history of the patriarchs, and of the wanderings in the desert will become a mere series of myths and popular legends. Israel, according to our newest lights, has no history before its settlement in Canaan.

This, then, is the latest pronouncement of the Higher Criticism. The Pentateuch, along with the Book of Joshua, is a sort of literary hash; hardly a fragment of it was in existence before the days of Josiah; and the history which twenty centuries have believed they found in it is little more than a delusion and a fraud. Israel and its religion lose the background of their history; and the only part of the Old Testament Scriptures which was received by the Samaritans as of supernatural origin, and to which the Jewish Church attached a special sanctity, is made later in date and inferior in veracity to a considerable part of the rest of the Old Testament canon.

Such revolutionary doctrines require a good deal of evidence to support them. But what do we actually find? Primarily an "analysis" by certain Western scholars in the nineteenth century of what are alleged to be the original elements of the text. The whole of the Pentateuch is sliced up into minute fragments, each of which is ticketed with a kind of algebraic symbol. The beginning of a verse is ascribed to one writer or "source," the middle of it to another, the end of it to a third. The critic knows exactly what each author wrote or pieced together, where "J" and "E" dovetail into one another, or where "P" breaks off and "D" commences. That this should sometimes happen in the middle of a sentence is of little consequence. The critic is as cocksure of his analysis as he is of the approximate age to which each writer or redactor should be assigned. A "polychromatic edition of the Old Testament" is even being published in America, in which the "eminent biblical scholars of Europe and America" exhaust all the colors of the rainbow in the effort to represent the literary mosaic work of the ancient Hebrew books.

Surely I am right in saying that such criticism is extravagant. Conceive of a similar "analysis" being applied to any English book, say of the Elizabethan era. Even in the case of a modern English work, like a novel of Besant and Rice, where we know that there is a dual authorship, the attempt to separate and distinguish between the two authors would be futile and impossible. And yet English is a language which we all speak and profess to know, and English literature is almost limitless in extent. The student of the Old Testament is in a very different position. The Hebrew literature that has come down to him is but a fragment of what once existed, and the interpretation of a good deal of it is doubtful. Our knowledge of the Hebrew language is in the highest degree imperfect; our Hebrew lexicons contain but a fraction of the words once possessed by it, and the meaning of many of the words which have been preserved, as well as of the idioms of the grammar, is merely a matter of conjecture. When we add to this that the critics are Europeans or Americans, whose training and modes of thought are utterly alien from those of the East, we may well come to the conclusion that the boasted "analysis" of the Pentateuch is but an ingenious way of weaving ropes out of the sand.

Yet this is the result in which years of learned labor and acute investigation have landed the "critic." We have, therefore, good reason for doubting the adequacy or legitimacy of his method. A method which leads us to a conclusion which is condemned by common sense cannot be a sound one. And a little consideration will show that it is not.

The counter-proof presented by archæology is of three kinds. First of all we have learned not only that Moses *could* have written the Pentateuch, but that it would have been something like a miracle if he had not done so. We have long known that the use of writing for literary purposes is immensely old in both Egypt and Babylonia. Egypt was emphatically a land of scribes and readers, and so, too, was Babylonia. Already, in the days of the Old Empire, the Egyptian hieroglyphs have developed into a cursive hand, while the Babylonian cities had their libraries of clay books centuries before the Bible tells us that Abraham was born in Ur of the Chaldees. But we now know a good deal more than this. Thanks to the discovery of the cuneiform tablets of Tel-el-Amarna in Upper Egypt, we now know that in the century before the exodus people were reading and writing and corresponding with one another throughout the civilized East, from the banks of the Euphrates to those of the Nile. And this was not all. The correspondence was carried on in the cuneiform characters, and for the most part in the language of Babylonia, necessitating the existence of schools where the foreign language and script could be taught and learned. What this means can be realized only by those who have studied the vast and complicated Babylonia syllabary, with the two languages, Semitic and Sumerian, which a knowledge of it implies. The center of all this literary activity was Canaan. At one time that country had been under the influence and domination of Babylonia, but in the age of the Tel-el-Amarna letters it had become an Egyptian province. A considerable number of the letters were written by Canaanites, and they show that a knowledge of reading and writing must have been widely spread throughout the land. Libraries and archive chambers existed, like those of Babylonia, and editions of Babylonian literary works were made for them. In fact, Canaan, in the

Mosaic age, like the countries which surrounded it, was fully as literary as was Europe in the time of *Renaissance*.

Can we imagine that in the midst of all this literary knowledge and activity the Israelites alone should have remained illiterate? To suppose, as my friend Dr. Neubauer puts it, that they alone were asleep while the rest of the world in which they lived was wide awake, is to conjure up a miracle greater than any of those which the traditional view of the Old Testament Scriptures calls upon us to believe. And if it is alleged that Moses did, indeed, write a Pentateuch, but that it has disappeared with the exception of a few tattered fragments in the Book of Exodus, we may reasonably ask what became of it, and why should the contemporaneous history it recorded have been superseded by the myths and legends of a later day? The Higher Criticism asserts that there was no writing, and, therefore, no history, in Israel before the age of Samuel. Oriental archæology, with no less emphasis, maintains that the Israelites must have known how to read and write before their settlement in Canaan.

Secondly, a study of the literature handed down to us by the Babylonian and Assyrian kinsfolk of the Israelites tells strongly against the disintegration theory of the Bible critics. We find in it no such slicing and fixing together of ill-assorted fragments as has been discovered in the Pentateuch. There were no redactors in Assyria and Babylon, with scissors and paste and the apparatus of a modern German study. Older materials were indeed used, but they were used as similar materials were by the Arabic writers of the Middle Ages, or by Herodotus at an earlier time. Either they were assimilated and thrown into shape by the author of the work which has come down to us, or passages were quoted faithfully from them and embodied in his narrative. Of slicing and patching there is no trace. And the faithfulness of the copies is astonishing. Where a word or character has been lost in the original tablet the copyist is careful to state there is a " lacuna " or a " recent lacuna ;" where the form of the original character was doubtful each of its possible later representatives is given. Even the compiler of the Babylonian Chronicle, in describing the great battle of Khalule, which laid

Babylonia at the feet of Sennacherib, candidly confesses that he does "not know the year" when it took place, although the inscriptions already in our hands, fewer though they are than those at his disposal, enable us to fix it with fair exactitude. But as no positive statement of the matter lay before him, the chronicler earnestly avows his ignorance. This was the way in which history was written among the Babylonian kinsmen of the Jews. After this, is it surprising that my brother Assyriologist, the illustrious Orientalist, Prof. Hommel, should declare his belief in the literary honesty of the Pentateuch, or should maintain that while there is evidence of the use of older documents in the Book of Genesis, it passes the wit of man to separate and distinguish them? The evidence for their existence is historical, and not linguistic.

Thirdly, the narratives which the Higher Criticism had pronounced to be the unhistorical figments of popular tradition are being shown by archæological discovery to be historical after all. Contemporaneous monuments are continually coming to light, which prove that in the story of the patriarchs and of the exodus we have truth and not legend. The Higher Criticism was triumphant only so long as the scientific instrument of comparison could not be employed against it.

I have dealt elsewhere with the monumental corroboration of the histories we find in the Pentateuch. Here I have no space to do more than refer to them, and to emphasize the fact that the most uncompromising opponents of the results of the Higher Criticism are to be found in the ranks of the foremost students of Assyrian and Egyptian antiquity. In truth, those of us who have devoted our lives to the archæology of the ancient Oriental world have been forced back into the traditional position, though doubtless with a broader basis to stand upon and clearer views of the real signification of the Biblical text. Year by year, almost month by month, fresh discoveries are breaking in upon us, each more marvelous than the last, but all, as regards the Pentateuch, in favor of the old, rather than of the new teaching. The story of the campaign of Chedor-laomer and his Babylonian allies against the Canaanitish princes has been fully confirmed, and now Mr. Pinches has found the name of Kudur-lagamar, or Chedor-laomer, as well as that of his ally, Tudghal, or Tidal. That Canaan was overrun by Babylonian arms and influence long before the age of Abraham was already known. This summer Prof. Hommel has discovered that Ine Sin, who ruled over Ur of the Chaldees centuries before the Hebrew patriarch was born there, captured the city of Zemar, in Phœnicia, while his daughter was high priestess of Anzan, or Elam, and of Northern Syria. Contract tablets, drawn up and dated in the reigns of Eri-Aku, or Arioch of Ellasar, and of other Babylonian kings of the same period, contain Hebrew names which indicate that a Hebrew-speaking population was settled in Babylonia at the time. Nay, more, the names of the Hebrew patriarchs, Abram, Jacob (-el) and Joseph (-el) have actually been met with by Mr. Pinches among those of witnesses to the deeds, while the kings of the dynasty which was governing Ur in the age of Chedor-laomer and Arioch bear names which are not Babylonian, but which are at once Hebrew and South Arabian. What a commentary this is upon the statement of Genesis that Eber begat two sons, one of whom was the ancestor of the Hebrew patriarchs, the other of the tribes of Southern Arabia!

But Oriental archæology can go further than prove that Moses could, after all, have written the Pentateuch, and that the narratives contained in it are derived from documents contemporaneous with the events they record. It can further show that there is no one else so likely to have written it as the great leader and legislator of Israel, to whom after ages agreed in ascribing the written law. Let us take, for example, the tenth chapter of Genesis, in which the geography of the Oriental world is described. There we are told that Canaan was the brother of Mizraim, or Egypt. The assertion was strictly true as long as Canaan was a province of Egypt; when it ceased to be so the statement was not only true no longer, it was contrary to the daily experience and political beliefs of every inhabitant of Palestine. But it was only during the rule of the eighteenth and nineteenth Egyptian dynasties that Canaan obeyed the government of the Pharaohs. With the fall of the nineteenth dynasty it was separated from the monarchy on the Nile, not to be again united to it, except during the short space of years that followed the death of Josiah. After the Mosaic age we cannot conceive of a writer coupling Canaan and Egypt together.

If, then, I were to be asked if I believe that Moses wrote the Pentateuch, I should answer that such a belief seems to me to involve considerably fewer difficulties than does the contrary belief of the Higher Criticism. Of course such a belief does not necessarily mean that the Hebrew legislator wrote the Pentateuch precisely in the form in which we now possess it. It does not exclude the fact of later revisions or the addition of editorial notes. Jewish tradition avers that in its present form the Pentateuch has come to us from Ezra and the men of the great Synagogue, and the doubts that have been cast upon the tradition savor of hypercriticism. But I see no reason for denying that the Pentateuch is substantially the work of Moses.

And against the counter-evidence of archæology what has the Higher Criticism to bring forward? Merely linguistic arguments. Lists of words and expressions have been compiled from the imperfect literature of an imperfectly known language, and interpreted by modern Europeans in accordance with certain documentary hypotheses. I have been a student of language and languages all my life, and the study has made me very skeptical as to the historical and literary conclusions that can be drawn from linguistic testimony alone. When we endeavor to extract other than linguistic conclusions from linguistic premises we generally go astray.

But even if the archæological and linguistic evidence should be held to neutralize one another, there is one tremendous fact to which the Higher Critics in this country resolutely close their eyes, but which ought to be more than sufficient to weigh down all the lists of words and idioms that were ever marshaled together. Against the evidence of the lists is the evidence of the doctrine and tradition of the Christian Church throughout the eighteen centuries of its existence. And those of us who believe that, in accordance with the promise of its divine Founder, the Spirit of God has been in the Church, guiding it into "all truth," find it impossible to believe at the same time that our new teachers can be right. The same method and arguments which have made of the Pentateuch a later and untrustworthy compilation, whose divine origin and character are discernible only to the critics themselves, would, if applied to the Gospels, end in the same results. In this country, it is true, our critical friends have hitherto kept their faces steadily averted from the New Testament, but the Protestant critics of the Continent have been less timid or prudent, and the way along which they should walk has long ago been pointed out to them by the Tübingen school. And even if we confine ourselves to the Pentateuch, the consequences of the "critical" position are serious enough. It is not only that the conception of the Mosaic law which lies at the back of our own religion, which was assumed by our Lord and his apostles, and which has been held ever since by the Christian Church, is swallowed up in chaotic darkness; we are forced to assign the origin of the belief in the divine message and supernatural authority of the law to successful fraud. I know we are told that what would be fraud in modern Europe was not fraud in ancient Israel, and that with an improvement in manners and education has come an improvement in morals. But the question is not about ancient Israel and its ideas of morality, but about the immutable God, under whose inspiration, if we are to follow the teaching of Christ and Christianity, the law was given to Israel. The Higher Critics never seem to me to realize that their conclusions are opposed to the great practical fact of the existence of traditional Christianity, and that against this fact they have nothing to set except the linguistic speculations of a few individual scholars. It is not Athanasius against the world, but Nestorius against the Church. On the one side we have a body of doctrine, which has been the support in life and the refuge in death of millions of men of all nationalities and grades of mind, which has been witnessed to by saints and martyrs, which has conquered first the Roman Empire and then the barbarians who destroyed it, and which has brought a message of peace and good will to suffering humanity. On the other side there is a handful of critics, with their lists of words and polychromatic Bibles. And yet the Higher Criticism has never saved any souls or healed any bodies.

Why is it so few of our religious periodicals have even noticed this most important testimony of this most eminent archæologist, supported as it is by Prof. Hommel, the illustrious Orientalist, and all of the foremost students of Assyrian and Egyptian antiquity? Is it not strikingly significant? Had Prof. Sayce's testimony been favorable to the Higher Criticism, would not our Church papers and magazines that now ignore this testimony have noticed it and given it much space? The critics say we are seeking light, and yet they close their eyes and turn from this light that shines as brightly as the noonday. They seem now rather to be defending their " Dearly bought scientific method," as Kuenen puts it, than seeking confirmations of the truth of God's holy Word.

CHAPTER XX.

THE JEW AND THE BIBLE.

"Verily I say unto you, This generation shall not pass, till all these things be fulfilled" (Matt. 24: 34).

The things mentioned in this passage are the surprising and extraordinary events with which "this present evil world" (*aion*) shall be terminated.

The word "generation" signifies the Jewish people. Webster defines it as "A family, a race, a stock, a breed." That these definitions are good is evident from Psalm 12: 7; 14: 5; 22: 30; 78: 15; and 112: 2. Also Luke 16: 8, and 1 Peter 2: 9.

The word *genea*, which is here rendered generation, is rendered "time" in Acts 14: 16, and 15: 21; "ages" in Eph. 3: 3, 31; and "nation" in Phil. 2: 15.

Dr. Charles Hodge says: "There is high authority for making 'this generation' here and in the parallel passages. Mark 13: 30, and Luke 21: 32, refer to Israel as a people or race; in this case the meaning would be that the Jews would not cease to be a distinct people until his predictions were fulfilled." (Systematic Theology, vol. 3, p. 799.)

Peter the Great once asked his chaplain to give him "one word" that would prove the religion of the Bible to be divine. After a few moments' reflection the chaplain replied, "Israel!" The king said, "I will think about it." Some days afterward he met the chaplain and said, "Your word is altogether convincing!" The great monarch was quite familiar enough with the laws and history of nations to know that Israel's preservation could not be accounted for except upon the ground of divine interposition.

All the great nations contemporaneous with Israel's earliest history, such as Egypt, Assyria, and Babylon; and the later great nations, as Greece and Rome, lie buried under the dust of centuries. But Israel, though scattered among the nations since the Maccabean reign, and persecuted and oppressed in the most cruel and atrocious manner, still preserves, amidst all the social, religious, and political convulsions of these centuries, her distinguishing peculiarities and characteristics as a people.

The apostle Paul in writing to the Romans asks the question, "What advantage, then, hath the Jew?" and then answers in these words, "Chiefly because that unto them were committed the oracles of God" (Rom. 3: 1, 2). We are here informed that the Jews are the custodians of the sacred oracles. "The word of the Lord endureth forever." See 1 Peter 1: 23-25, and Isa. 40: 6-8. Since the Word of God is to stand forever, its custodians must also be preserved. This wonderful people shall not cease to exist, as such, until all the wonderful things predicted in this wonderful Book, for this age, are consummated. A people divinely chosen and miraculously preserved for the purpose of preserving the God-given Book. "For I could wish that I myself were anathema from Christ for my brethren's sake, my kinsmen according to the flesh: who are Israelites; whose is the adoption, and the glory, and the covenants [testaments], and the giving of the law, and the service of God, and the promises; whose are the fathers, and of whom is Christ as concerning the flesh, who is over all, God blessed forever. Amen" (Rom. 9: 3-5).

www.ingramcontent.com/pod-product-compliance
Lightning Source LLC
Chambersburg PA
CBHW021410230426
43666CB00006B/704